WHERE

A Family Book of Knowledge

octopus
Octopus Books

ABOUT THIS BOOK

Life consists of asking questions. We start from the moment we learn to string words together and most of us go on asking them for the rest of our lives. Alas, we don't always find the answers. This book (and its companion volumes in this series) presents a random array of questions most commonly asked—and not only by children. When a question springs to mind, ferreting out the answer can be a difficult business. Often the answer lies buried in a mass of information we don't need. These books go straight to the heart of the matter and answer simple (and not so simple) questions in a down-to-earth manner. Where does the word "ambergris" come from? Where do elephants die? Where was the first bicycle made? Where do dreams and shadows go to? The questions are divided into six

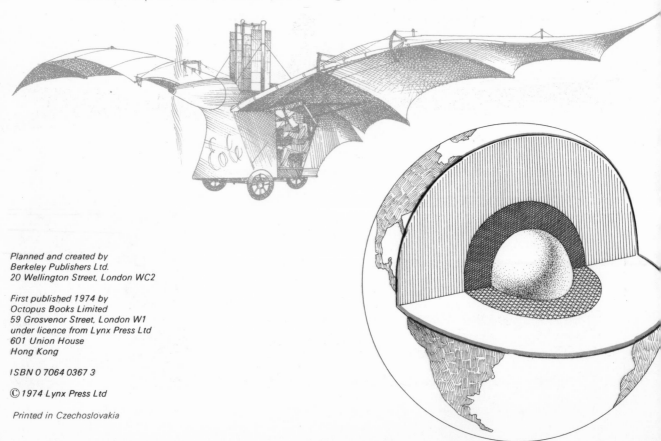

Planned and created by
Berkeley Publishers Ltd.
20 Wellington Street, London WC2

First published 1974 by
Octopus Books Limited
59 Grosvenor Street, London W1
under licence from Lynx Press Ltd
601 Union House
Hong Kong

ISBN 0 7064 0367 3

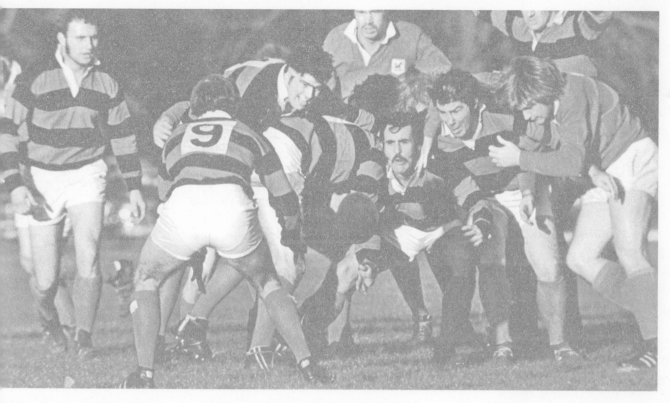

main categories. There is no attempt to be definitive,

for millions of questions could be posed. With the help of a team of teachers

and students, we've picked out the ones

most commonly asked—and some that simply appeal to us.

If you know that the highest tide in the world is recorded in

the Bay of Fundy, if you can instantly put a name to the largest

island in the world or the greatest ocean

depth, then go to the top of the question class.

If you can't, then welcome aboard. Our family

book of questions will be your perfect guide and

companion. If you can't find the answer

to your own particular pet questions in WHERE?,

well then, try WHEN? or WHAT? or WHY?

And when you've exhausted *our* questions, try

dreaming up some of your own—and find out the answers for yourself!

IN THIS BOOK

Natural History

People and Events

The Body and Medicine

Geography and the Earth

Science and Technology

General Knowledge

Natural History

lar is the tiger cowrie. The shell grows about four inches long and is covered with spots. It was used by 18th Century silversmiths to make shell snuff-boxes and in Italy for burnishing paper and ironing lace. The shells were often distributed in Europe by sailors and gypsies.

Orange cowries at one time sold for large sums on the market. In Fiji and the New Hebrides in the Pacific they are still worn as badges of rank by the chiefs.

The money cowrie is a small oval shell, flat and white underneath with thick yellowish-white edges and a pale lemon upper surface. It is found in enormous quantities in the Pacific, from the Moluccas eastward. Large fortunes were at one time made by European traders who transported shells to the west coast of Africa and exchanged them for ivory,

COWRIE SHELLS

Cowrie shells are widely distributed and possibly the favourites among shell collectors because of their polished enamel-like surfaces and their beautiful coloured patterns. The cowrie appears in all the warmer seas of the globe. But the great cowries, the tiger cowrie and the orange cowrie are natives of tropical regions. They crawl slowly, browsing on weeds, and are shy creatures remaining hidden during the day in crevices or under rocks.

The best-known and most popu-

breadfruit tree?

gold and slaves. A slave would be worth anything from 20,000 to 50,000 shells. In 1849 money cowries weighing 240 tons were imported into the English port of Liverpool.

A man at Cuttack in Orissa, India, paid for the erection of his bungalow entirely in cowries. The building cost him £400, which in cowries amounted to 16,000,000 shells. The common method of handling the cowries was by threading them on a string, 40 cowries to one string.

Among the cowries the rarest is *Cypreae leucedon*. Only two known examples of this pale brown, creamy-spotted shell exist. One is in the British Museum, the other in the Harvard University Museum. More than 190 species of cowrie shell are known to collectors. Some species are used as charms against evil spirits.

BREADFRUIT TREE

The breadfruit tree is found in the South Pacific islands and, to a lesser degree, in other parts of the tropics. It is an extremely handsome tree, growing up to 60 feet high. The oval leaves are a pleasant, glossy green and quite large.

There are two distinct forms of breadfruit, one seedless and the other containing many seeds which, when boiled or roasted, taste much like chestnuts.

The breadfruit, which contains a considerable amount of starch, is not really a fruit in the popular sense and is rarely eaten raw. It can be boiled or baked, served with salt, butter or syrup, and even sliced and fried like potatoes.

The tree has been cultivated in Malaya since remote antiquity. It can also be found in the West Indies where Captain Bligh, of H.M.S. Bounty, introduced it on a later voyage.

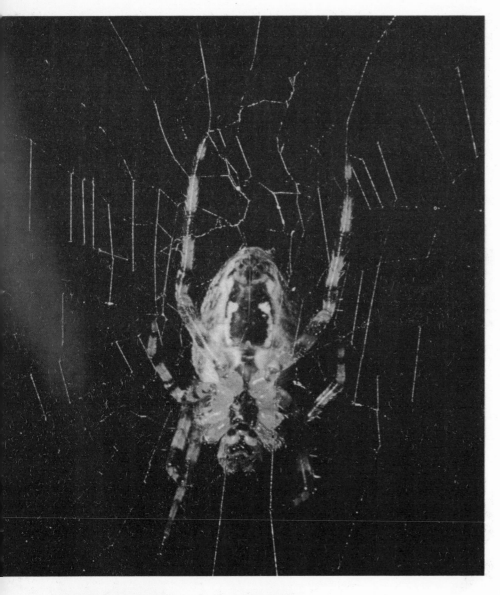

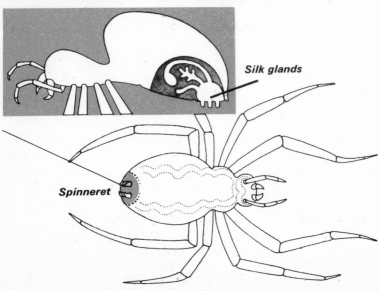

Silk glands

Spinneret

SPIDER'S WEB

A spider does not have a ready-made web. She spins one. If you are lucky, you may be able to watch the female spider doing this.

The material that makes the thread for the spider's web is a liquid which she produces from tiny spinning tubes. These spinning tubes are to be found on small lumps on her body, known as spinnerets. As soon as the liquid comes into the air, it hardens and changes into thread.

When a spider sets out to spin a web she first uses a tough thread to build an outer frame in which she fits spokes, as in a wheel. Next she starts from the hub to weave a spiral crossing the spokes about five times, just to keep them in position. Then she begins again at the outside rim to spin a complete spiral with finer silk, cutting away the "scaffolding" as she nears the centre. Finally she constructs new support-lines for the finished web.

When the spiders move they spin out lines behind them. These are known as the "draglines", and spiders use them as anchors. They do this by pressing their spinnerets against small objects like pebbles or plants. These are the most important threads of all.

Spiders use their webs for trapping flies and other insects to eat. So, besides being beautiful to look at, spiders' webs are vital to them as food providers.

FIRST ZOO

The first zoo was formed in China in the 12th Century B.C. But it was not called a zoo. Wen, the ancient Chinese king who started it, wanted to collect different types of animals from all over his empire. He kept them in what he called a "garden of intelligence", near his palace.

Some of the largest zoos are in North America. There are big ones in the Bronx, New York City, and in Washington and San Diego.

too? WHERE does a swallow nest?

SWALLOW'S NEST

A swallow builds its nest inside farm buildings and on ledges in old chimneys. The nest is made of mud, straw and saliva, with feathers and wool to line the inside. It takes a pair of swallows up to several weeks to make the saucer-shaped nest in the rafters of a barn.

Swallows start arriving in Europe at the end of March, a little earlier than their close relatives, the house martins. They spend the winter in South Africa and usually return to the same district—and even the same nest—where they settled before. The female lays four or five eggs, white with reddish-brown speckles. She sits on them for about 15 days before they hatch out. Both parents then feed the nestlings with insects which they catch while flying. Swallows usually lay two sets of eggs.

They leave for their winter quarters in September, gathering in large flocks and often perching on telephone wires, before setting off. The young birds of the first brood leave before their parents and, by an inborn knowledge, know which way to go.

An old country proverb says: "One swallow does not make a summer". This means that when the first one or two swallows arrive, summer has not yet come. It is not until large flocks are seen that countrymen know they can expect the warmer weather.

WHERE are crocodiles born?   WHERE would you look fo

CROCODILES

A newly-hatched crocodile is about eight inches long and can be found on the mud near the water's edge of marshes, rivers, estuaries and lakes around the tropical regions of the world. For it is here that the female lays her eggs and buries them—30 to 70 at a time—in holes in the warm mud.

Each of the hard-shelled eggs is about the size of a goose's egg. After being covered by vegetation which, as it rots, supplements the warmth of the sun, the batch is guarded by the female until the eggs are about to hatch. Then the crocodile digs down to free them from the mud.

Adult crocodiles vary in size from the three-feet-long dwarf ones of West Africa to those in the estuaries of tropical Asia and Australia which can attain a length of 20 feet.

These salt-water estuary crocodiles, including those that live in the tidal part of the River Nile in North Africa, are occasionally man-eaters and will attack and eat almost any living creature that comes within their reach. They were once thought to weep as they snapped up their victim. That is why in popular speech we often describe a false display of sorrow as "crocodile tears".

baobab tree? **WHERE** does a leech feed?

LEECH

Leeches, which are rather slimy worms and vary in length from an inch to several inches, have two suckers, a big one at the rear and a smaller one at the mouth end. They have powerful muscles which enable them to expand and contract their bodies.

This makes them excellent swimmers. They can also use their suckers to crawl on the land. In tropical Asia, the islands of the Pacific and the Indian ocean, there is a particularly vicious and dreaded species of land leech which enters the breathing passages of animals, gorges on the animal's blood and swells so that it cannot escape.

Aquatic or water leeches cling to fishes, turtles and shell fish. Some leeches feed on earthworms and frogs' eggs. Others live on the larvae of insects and even on the microscopic life on the floor of the pond.

Leeches have been used in medicine from early times until quite recently to draw blood from a patient. They also serve as fish bait. In parts of the United States they are regarded as useful in controlling the snail population in lakes and ponds.

BAOBAB TREE

The baobab tree is to be found in tropical Africa. It is a most strange-looking tree. Its barrel-like trunk can reach 30 feet or more in diameter, although its height is not proportionately great.

It has a large gourd-like, woody, fruit containing a pleasant, cool tasting juice. A strong fibre obtained from the bark is used in Africa to make ropes and cloth. The wood is soft and light and so easy to work that the trunks of living trees are often excavated to form houses.

So peculiar is the baobab in appearance that an Arabian legend says: "The devil plucked up the baobab, thrust its branches into the earth, and left its roots in the air".

A related species is found in Australia, where it is also known as the bottle tree.

WHERE do ostriches nest? WHERE do salmon go to breed

OSTRICH NESTS

We all know that birds build nests. Some find trees the most convenient. Others prefer hedges, the eaves of roofs, chimney pots, rocky ledges or holes in trees. But what does a bird do that can neither fly nor swim?

Living on the dry, open plains of eastern and southern Africa, the ostrich takes no pains to hide its nest. It merely finds a suitable shallow depression in the ground, which it may scoop out further with its feet. The hole may be up to three yards across. In it are laid six to eight eggs, each one by a different female. Then one hen and one cock take turns guarding the two and a half pound eggs until they are ready to hatch.

However, the ostrich does not sit on its eggs to incubate them. Rather, it squats between them, spreading its wings to provide shade and keep them from cooking in the hot desert sun. With one bird squatting and the other standing guard, there is little chance that any smaller egg-eating mammal or bird will find a meal.

WHERE would you look for a trap-door spider?

SALMON

Atlantic salmon, called the "greatest game fish in the world" by sportsmen, spawn in the freshwater streams of Europe, from Portugal to northern Russia, and in the streams of the eastern seaboard of North America, from Maine up to northern Canada. They are found also in the streams of Greenland and Iceland.

Pacific salmon, of which there are several kinds, spawn in the streams of southern Alaska, British Columbia and the states of Washington and Oregon on the Pacific coast. There is also one kind which breeds in the streams of Russia's east coast.

The females spawn their thousands of eggs and the males fertilize them. Once the Pacific female salmon have spawned they die. The eggs hatch in about 19 weeks. The tiny salmon called an "alevin" hides in the gravelly bed of the stream, living at first on a large yolk-sac under its body. When about a year old it is called a "parr" and looks like a young trout. Six months later when it has a more salmony look it is called a "smolt". On reaching the sea it becomes a "grilse" until it reaches maturity.

The instinct of the salmon to head for the sea after a couple of years in fresh water is one of the great mysteries of nature. So too is its instinct, after ranging the Atlantic and Pacific Oceans and travelling up to 4,000 miles, to return to spawn in the stream where its own life began.

TRAP-DOOR SPIDER

Trap-door spiders are to be found just under the surface of the earth. They belong to the class of spiders called *mygalomorphae* which includes the bird-eating spiders of the tropics. All these spiders tend to be rather large. They have four lungs instead of two, and their jaws work vertically instead of sideways.

The trap-door spider has perfected the art of burrowing underground. Its jaws are provided with a special row of teeth with which to dig out its home. It lines its burrow with silk and makes a trap-door consisting of layers of silk and earth. The outside of this door is coated with moss or some other form of camouflage. The spider lies in wait behind its trap-door, darting out to seize its prey.

Trap-door spiders are widespread throughout the hottest regions of the world, with comparatively few in the temperate zones. Specimens of up to four and a half inches have been found. It is estimated that some may live up to 20 years.

WHERE do elephants die? WHERE do sponges come from

ELEPHANTS

Groups of elephants have been found buried together both in Africa and Asia. The nearness of the animals to each other may be no more than a coincidence. The areas may be no more than sites, since elevated and dried, where elephants have been drowned in bogs or while crossing rivers.

However, many people will argue that old elephants, when their end is near, resort to their legendary "graveyards". The discovery of the remains of a solitary elephant is rare. On the other hand a body in elephant country would usually soon disappear owing to the activities of natural scavengers.

Most experts will accept that there is much truth in the old saying "an elephant never forgets". It does have a retentive memory. Also, when an elephant is dying it is not uncommon for members of the herd to gather round and try to revive it. When all hope is lost they encircle their relation as if in mourning at a funeral.

LONGEST SNAKE

The longest snake in the world—the python—is found in the tropics, in and around the Malay region. It is the reticulated or regal python, which can sometimes be as much as 30 feet long. It kills its prey by coiling itself round the animal and hugging it, so that it cannot breathe. Then it swallows the victim whole.

The python is strong enough to kill an ox, but chooses smaller animals which it can swallow. If a python is disturbed soon after a meal, it is likely to vomit the animal up again, still whole. It rarely attacks man and is not poisonous.

Most pythons live in trees. They also like lying in water where it is cool.

The python lays oval eggs with leathery shells, sometimes as many as 100 at a time. It guards the eggs by coiling itself round them.

The anaconda, which inhabits the rivers and swamps of Brazil, Peru and the Guianas is the largest American snake; it rivals and sometimes exceeds the python in size.

SPONGES

The soft, absorbent, natural sponges used in baths are the skeletal remains of a marine animal. Biologists once thought sponges were plants. This seemed natural as sponges have no special shape and attach themselves to one spot on the sea-bed like plants. Also, they have no limbs, mouths or internal organs. Today, however, they are classified as animals.

The familiar commercial sponges are gathered by divers or by dredging ships. They are prised from the sea floor and dried in the sun. After any impurities have been washed out of the sponge, it is ready to be sold in the market. Some of the best sponges are found off the coasts of Turkey, Greece and Egypt.

WHERE is the longest snake in the world?

THE DODO

The dodo was rather a stupid bird. Indeed, it was so stupid that it was named dodo by the Portuguese when they discovered Mauritius— its home—in 1507. The Portuguese word *doudo* means stupid.

Mauritius is an island, 720 square miles in area and lying 500 miles to the east of Madagascar in the Indian Ocean. Until the arrival of man, with his attendant creatures such as the cat and dog, the dodo had been able to live in peace. It had no enemies, which was fortunate because it was big and clumsy and was completely unsuited to fleeing from danger. Its short legs were almost incapable of supporting the weight of the fat, round body (about the size of a swan's), and the ridiculously inadequate, stubby wings were of no use for flying.

Within 180 years of its discovery by the Portuguese, the dodo was extinct. Over the intervening years several were brought to Europe alive, and one was to be seen in London in 1638. By 1680 the dodo had succumbed.

With the help of drawings and by the collection of bones gathered in Mauritius, an almost complete reconstruction has been made of the poor bird. It can be seen at the Natural History Museum in London.

Mauritius is the only place in the world where the bird is known to have existed. A similar bird once lived on the neighbouring island of Rodriguez, but this also has become extinct.

The phrase "as dead as the dodo" is used to mean that something is very dead indeed.

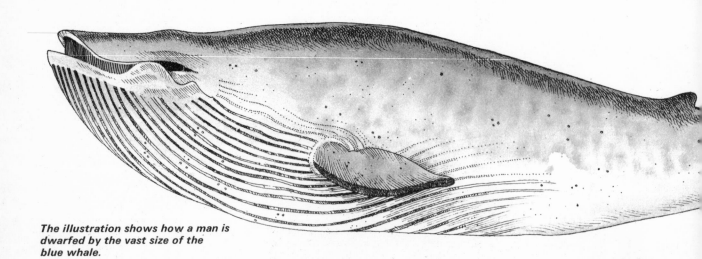

The illustration shows how a man is dwarfed by the vast size of the blue whale.

LARGEST ANIMAL

Blue whales are the largest living animals. They are cosmopolitan creatures and are found in most of the seas, from the polar caps to the equator. Normally those which inhabit the colder seas will migrate to warmer waters in winter.

Their dimensions are almost beyond belief. Although figures can never be quite accurate, a blue whale can weigh more than 200 tons and many have been found measuring over 100 feet in length. The tongue alone, of a female whale found in Antarctica, weighed well over four tons.

It has been estimated that in the 1930s there were nearly 40,000

world's largest animal?   **WHERE** does a bee keep its sting?
WHERE would you find truffles?

BEE STING

A bee keeps its sting at the end of its abdomen. At the tip of a bee's abdomen is a shaft where its stinging thorn is to be found. It can sting several times, but once it leaves the thorn in its victim's flesh it will not be able to sting again.

It is not true to say that a bee will automatically die once it loses its thorn. Only female bees can sting. Male bees, or drones, lack this means of protecting themselves.

There is a species of which even the female cannot sting. But these bees which live mainly in Africa and South America are not defenceless. If disturbed, they will fly at the intruder in great numbers, crawl into his eyes, ears and hair and smear him with a sticky substance, causing him to retreat in great discomfort.

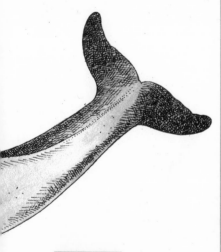

Approx 5′ 8″

blue whales in the world. But by the end of the 1960s there were fewer than 1,000 alive. This was because they became popular victims for the misdirected efforts of over-zealous hunters.

TRUFFLES

If you want to sound extremely clever you can confuse your friends by telling them that the real name for truffles is Ascomycetes. That's what the botanists call them. But you're most likely to come across truffles in the very best French pâtés—for example, in the famous pâtés of the Perigord region of France.

The Perigord truffles became famous for culinary purposes as long ago as the 15th Century and ever since that time they have been regarded as essential to the production of the very finest pâtés.

These Perigord truffles have a distinct smell, but this is by no means unpleasant. Some truffle hunters can actually smell out the truffle in the woodlands but in France specially trained hounds with a keenly developed sense of smell are used.

Truffles look rather like large spongy walnuts and they grow under the soil. Pigs adore them. In early days pigs were turned loose in the woodlands to root for the truffles buried beneath the soil and leaves. Even today pigs are used to sniff out truffles but they certainly are not allowed to eat them, since truffles fetch high prices as a food delicacy.

The best truffles are considered to be those in the forest regions of the Dordogne area of France, where the climate is warm and moist, and there is plenty of limestone in the earth. This is one reason why Perigord, in the heart of the Dordogne, has achieved such a great reputation for fine pâtés. The most famous pâté of all —the very expensive *pâté de foie gras*—comes from Perigord.

Truffles are also found in the southern counties of France's neighbour, England. The commonest English truffle has the botanical name of *Tuber Aestivam*. It is found on chalky soil and in beech woods. In the county of Wiltshire these truffles are cropped commercially.

20

WHERE do you find frogs that live in trees? WHERE would

TREE-FROGS

Tree-frogs are found in Europe, North and South America, New Guinea, North Africa, and warm parts of Asia. They have small sticky discs on the tops of their fingers and toes which help them cling to the branches of trees.

The best-known European tree-frog is less than two inches long. Its Latin name is *Hyla arborea*. Its colour is usually bright green. But tree-frogs can change colour even as you watch them. They can become yellow, brown or black.

In North America there are two main types of tree-frog. One is called the spring peeper. It has a shrill piping voice. The other one is known as *Hyla versicolor*. Versicolor is a Latin word meaning "various colours". This frog can be grey, green or brown. It has a loud croaking voice.

PEARLS

Pearls come from molluscs—a group of animals which includes squids, clams, and oysters.

Under its shell the mollusc has a mantle, or outer-skin. When a particle of dirt, or tiny marine creature gets stuck in this mantle, a hard substance forms around it. This makes the pearl. It is formed of the same material as the mollusc shell—nacre or mother-of-pearl.

Pearls come in many different shapes and colours. The most valuable ones are completely smooth, spherical and usually white. But there is a black pearl from the Gulf of Mexico, which is also extremely valuable.

The people who first discovered how to stimulate the production of pearls were the Chinese. They put the mollusc into a shallow pond, inserted a speck of mud into the mantle, and waited for the pearl to form. After a couple of months they would detach the pearl from the mollusc's mantle—and eat the mollusc.

ou find pearls? **WHERE** does lichen grow?

LICHEN

Lichens are found throughout the world, often occupying areas where no other plant can become established. They are found in their greatest numbers in the Alpine and Arctic regions, where they are the dominant form of vegetation.

Lichens are the products of two distinct groups of plants. Together fungi and algae (seaweed is an algae) combine to produce lichens. Most rocks you will come across have an abundance of these plants. Lichens are almost the only plants able to survive the severe conditions at high altitudes.

In Antarctica, where there are very few flowering plants, more than 400 species of lichens have been found. In warmer climates lichens are common in old fields and forests, on rotting logs and on tree trunks. However, few species survive near large cities. Unfortunately, lichens are very sensitive to industrial smoke and gases.

WHELKS

A whelk is a kind of sea-snail. It eats clams, worms, barnacles and smaller snails. The female lays her eggs in hard capsules. These are arranged in clusters of strings and attached to rock, wood, and shells.

Fishermen use whelks as bait. They catch the whelks by setting traps and baiting them with crabs.

Whelks are eaten by cod and starfish, the kind of fish that find their food at or near the bottom of the sea bed.

CAVIARE

Caviare is the roe of the female members of the sturgeon family. These fish are found in northern and central Asia, Europe and North America.

The best quality black caviare comes from sturgeon caught during the winter months in the estuaries of rivers which flow into the Baltic Sea. It is regarded as a great delicacy and has been known in western Europe since the sixteenth century. Shakespeare mentions it in his play *Hamlet*. In the Soviet Union and eastern Europe, the coarser quality caviare is a staple food and is traditionally accompanied by gulps of vodka.

When caviare is prepared, the roe is carefully strained to remove fibres and fat. It is then salted and packed into small barrels, jars or tins. Its salty flavour and grainy texture are an acquired taste. But like all expensive foods, it is a taste thought by many people to be worth acquiring. Caviare is usually served as an *hors d'oeuvre* with bread or toast, or on small biscuits with drinks.

As well as the grey and black caviare, there is also a red caviare. This is prepared from the roe of salmon and is considered by experts in these matters to be of inferior quality.

:ome from? **WHERE** do butterflies go when it rains?

BUTTERFLIES

When it rains butterflies settle on the stems of flowers or stalks of grass. They hang head downwards with their wings folded together over their backs. Most butterflies are difficult to see when their wings are closed, because the undersides have only pale colours and faint patterns.

There are about 10,000 known species of butterfly. They range in size from less than an inch to the swallow-tails which live in north Australia and the Pacific Islands and have a wing span of 10 inches. Most female butterflies have less colourful wings than the males of the same species. They lay between 100 and 3,000 eggs, according to the species, placing them on a plant which will provide suitable food for the caterpillars which develop from the eggs.

The caterpillar becomes a chrysalis from which, eventually, the fully grown butterfly emerges.

Adult life may last for only a few weeks, but some butterflies hibernate.

Butterflies feed on the nectar of plants and on sweet juices, particularly those of over-ripe or rotting fruit. This food provides them with the energy to fly but is not used for body-building. All growth takes place at the caterpillar stage of a butterfly's life.

A silver-studded blue butterfly

WHERE would you find a live prehistoric fish? WHERE do
WHERE does the word 'ambergris'

PREHISTORIC FISH

Numerous fossil remains have been found of coelacanth fish which died over 70 million years ago. In fact the coelacanth is said to have first appeared some 350 million years ago.

But to the amazement of experts the first living coelacanth was found in 1938 off the coast of South Africa. In 1952 a second one was caught on a line by a fisherman from the Comoro Islands, between Mozambique and Madagascar. Since then many more coelacanths have been taken around the Comoros.

Modern coelacanths are bigger than most of the fossil forms. They average about five feet in length and can weigh more than 100 pounds.

Usually they live among reefs, from which they will dart out on their prey. They are strong and powerful flesh eaters. The heart of a coelacanth is an S-shaped tube and is probably the most primitive of its kind in existence today.

FLIES

During winter flies will hibernate, sometimes in large groups, in any available dry and warm space such as an attic.

The reason there are so few houseflies in winter is that their eggs will hatch only at temperatures between 24° Centigrade and 35° Centigrade (75° Fahrenheit and 95° Fahrenheit). Meanwhile their numbers steadily diminish owing to insecticides and natural causes. This is a good thing since flies often carry diseases.

AMBERGRIS

The French words *ambre gris* mean grey amber, but amber bears no relation to ambergris. The first is derived from plants and the second from animals.

Amber is a yellowish, translucent fossil resin. Millions of years ago large heaps of resin which oozed from pine trees were buried by soil, and hardened into amber. Insects now extinct have been found preserved in these amber lumps. Amber is found chiefly along the southern shores of the Baltic Sea. It has long been used for making into beads and ornaments.

The Greeks and Romans believed that amber had special and mysterious powers because, when rubbed, it attracts light objects. The Greeks called it *elektron* from which the word electricity is derived.

Grey amber or ambergris is a secretion from the intestines of the spermaceti or sperm whale. It is a light, fatty substance, grey in colour and flecked like marble. It is sometimes found floating in large masses weighing as much as 200 pounds in tropical seas.

In ancient times ambergris was used as a scent. It is still used by modern scent manufacturers as a fixative in the making of perfumes.

lies go in the winter?
ome from? **WHERE** would you find a Red Giant?

RED GIANTS

You would find a Red Giant on the Sierra Nevada mountains of California in North America. It is a huge redwood tree, called a giant sequoia. These trees, members of the conifer family, are the largest in the world and grow to a height of 300 feet. They have a very hard, reddish brown wood and a thick, very rough bark. The giant sequoias were believed to be the oldest living things in the world. The ring marks on the stumps of the oldest trunks have been carefully counted and it is now known that some of the biggest are about 4,000 years old.

Many of these trees were cut down for their timber, which is resistant to attacks by fungus, and termites and other insects. To preserve the remaining groves of these huge redwoods, a reservation called the Sequoia National Park was set up in 1890. The largest tree there is 272 feet high and has a circumference at the base of its trunk of $101\frac{1}{2}$ feet. Its weight has been estimated to be over 6,000 tons.

Some of the other trees are taller but do not have such large trunks. A tunnel has been cut through the base of one of these giant trees which is big enough to drive a car through.

People and Events

JULIUS CAESAR

Julius Caesar landed in Britain on a low, shelving beach somewhere between the modern towns of Deal and Walmer in Kent.

Caesar decided to invade Britain when he was Proconsul in Gaul. Only vague ideas prevailed about the British islands, but they were known to be rich in tin. So, late in August 55 B.C., Caesar sailed across the channel with 80 transports and two legions. After a short, ferocious fight amid the waves, his men reached the shore and put the Britons to flight.

But Caesar's troubles had only just begun. His cavalry, in 18 transports, was caught in a sudden gale and driven back to Gaul, while the high tide battered the ships that lay at anchor. The Britons again attacked, were once more driven back and finally submitted. Caesar made no attempt to penetrate further inland and never even pretended that his expedition had been a success.

The following year he returned with five legions and some cavalry in 800 ships. He spent 10 days having all his ships hauled ashore. Then he crossed the River Thames near Brentford. The British had found a leader, Cassivelaunus, who harassed the Roman troops severely. Caesar was glad to negotiate with the British chieftain, to accept some hostages and tribute and then to quit the island.

For nearly 100 years no invading army landed again in Britain.

Julius Caesar (102-44 B.C.) was a member of a noble family but also became a favourite with the people of Rome. As Overseer of the Public Games in 65 B.C., he organized magnificent spectacles to win popularity, for he felt himself to be the man who would save Rome from decay. In 59 B.C. he was elected Consul and a year later was sent as Proconsul to Transalpine Gaul (now France).

Marx buried? WHERE are the Heights of Abraham?

KARL MARX

Karl Marx was buried in Highgate Cemetery in North London on 17 March, 1883. On his gravestone are carved these sentences from his works:

"The philosophers have only interpreted the world in various ways; the point, however, is to change it."

"Workers of all lands, unite."

Karl Marx had German-Jewish parents. He started work as a journalist, after attending university in Bonn, Berlin and Jena where he studied law, philosophy and history. When he was 25 his newspaper was closed down, and he left Germany in search of freedom. After being expelled from France he went to Brussels where with Frederick Engels he wrote *The Communist Manifesto.*

He eventually settled in England, where he lived with his family in poverty in Soho, London. It was here that he wrote his classic work *Das Kapital,* which describes in an historical setting the working of the capitalist system and what Marx felt would be its ultimate evolution into control of all the means of production and supply by the workers.

HEIGHTS OF ABRAHAM

These cliffs are one of the outstanding natural features of the city of Quebec in Canada and were the scene of a famous battle.

Major-General James Wolfe (1727-59) was only 32 years old when commanded by the British Prime Minister, William Pitt, to capture Quebec from the French during the Seven Years' War (1756-63). The capture of the city lying on the banks of the St Lawrence River in eastern Canada, would open the way for the overthrow of the French forces in North America.

For three months in the summer of 1759, Wolfe attempted to overcome the French by frontal attack from across the river, but the defenders held an almost impregnable position. Wolfe decided to make an attack from the rear. In the early, dark hours of September 13, he led his army across the river above the town and surprised the French soldiers guarding the small cove which now bears his name.

Then came the highly dangerous task of scaling the cliffs—the Heights of Abraham. By sunrise

Wolfe and his army of 4,000 had achieved their goal and were on the Plains of Abraham, drawn up in battle array and ready for battle.

Before Wolfe's audacious plan had been carried to its successful conclusion, both Wolfe and the great French commander, Montcalm, lay dying on the battlefield. Knowing that success was his, Wolfe whispered, "I die contented". On the other hand, when told that he was fatally wounded, Montcalm cried out: "Thank God! I shall not live to see the surrender of Quebec."

WHERE was Joan of Arc burned to death? WHERE did th

A painting in the Tassili Plateau caves, Algeria.

FIRST MEN

Our early ancestors in all lands made their first homes in the natural shelter provided by caves. In these primitive dwellings the caveman stored all his worldly belongings, his tools, weapons, ornaments, and the bones of the animals he killed. Many caves were decorated with fine but simple paintings and engravings on the rock surfaces, usually depicting animals and hunting scenes. Man, at the beginning of history, was a good gatherer depending for his survival on hunting wild animals and birds, fishing and collecting wild fruits, nuts and berries.

Nobody can be sure when man first started to use caves as shelter. But our history begins about 600,000 or 700,000 years ago, when our ancestors first started to make and use tools. From the remnants of these tools archaeologists and historians have been able to piece together the caveman's way of life.

Originally cavemen lived just with their families, but soon tribes were formed and bigger caves sought to house them all together. In Switzerland the Holloch cave extends for 38 miles and near Grenoble in France caves as deep as 3,000 feet have been found.

JOAN OF ARC

Joan of Arc, the peasant girl who led the French to victory at Orleans and Charles VII to his coronation at Rheims, was burned to death as a heretic by the English on May 31, 1431, in the Place du Vieux Marché in Rouen. Her great heroism and leadership, which she claimed to be inspired by the voices of three saints, played a decisive part in the revival of France at the crisis of the Hundred Years War against the English invaders.

Joan was born in 1412 at Domrémy, a village between Champagne and Lorraine on the banks of the Meuse. She led cattle to pasture and sang and danced with the other village girls until, at the age of 13, she began to hear voices and see visions. Later these voices urged her to go to Orleans and raise the siege of the city. With the approval of the Church she entered Orleans and defeated the besieging English.

After a famous battle at Patay in June, 1429, in which Joan led the French to a great victory, she persuaded Charles the Dauphin to go to Rheims where he was crowned king. Joan, the Maid of Orleans, stood near the altar during the ceremony, holding her banner aloft.

The Maid was captured by the Burgundians in a skirmish on May 30, 1430, and handed over to the Bishop of Beauvais. After an inquisition by the Church she was delivered to the English. To the very last moment of her ordeal she claimed that her voices were sent to her by God. The executioner later said that her heart would not burn and that he had found it intact in the ashes. This story became part of her legend.

rst men live ? **WHERE** did Buddha live ?

THE BUDDHA

Buddha's full name was Gautama Buddha, and he lived in north-east India. He was born into a warrior tribe called the Sakyas in the 6th Century B.C. and became the founder of the religion called Buddhism.

Although he was of noble birth, Buddha was not proud and fond of luxury. Even when young, he was serious and thought a great deal. He decided it was better to lead a humble, religious life.

When he was 29, he left his home and became a monk. He found strength in quiet meditation. He saw that the world was full of suffering, and wanted to help people. So he became a wandering teacher.

Buddha gave his first sermon at Benares on the River Ganges. Here, he outlined the beliefs which have guided Buddhists ever since. Buddha said first of all that worldly life cannot give final happiness. You should not be either completely self-indulgent or too strict with yourself. You should try to follow a middle path, maintaining inner peace and discipline. A Buddhist's final spiritual goal is a blissful state called Nirvana, in which he is completely calm and free from any pain or anxiety.

The name Buddha means "The Enlightened One". He died near Benares when he was 80. By then he had organized a community of monks, called the Sangha, to carry on his teachings.

The main countries where Buddhism is practised are Burma, Thailand, Ceylon and Japan. There are about 177,000 Buddhists in North America.

This magnificent gilt bronze figure of a seated Buddha comes from Nepal. It was made in the 15th Century. The position of the seated figure is typical of many statues of Buddha, of which there are a huge number.

WHERE did the American War of Independence start?
WHERE was the Klondike

WAR OF INDEPENDENCE

The American War of Independence started at Lexington, near Boston, Massachusetts, in 1775. The military governor of Massachusetts had sent troops from Boston to Concord to seize a store of illegal weapons. On the way back, at Lexington, the troops were attacked by angry farmers and 273 of the 800 soldiers were killed. When the news of this battle reached Britain, war was declared on the rebellious colonists.

Although this was the first open conflict, the colonists' resentment against Britain had been growing for several years. This was mainly caused by the taxes imposed by the British government on certain goods imported into America. The taxes were intended to help pay for the Seven Years' War which Britain had fought against France

to defend the American states. The Americans considered these taxes to be unjust and refused to pay them. Eventually all these taxes were abolished, except for the tax on imported tea.

When war was declared, the Americans had no regular army. But one was soon formed under the command of a Virginian, George Washington. This army was badly equipped and lacked training. But it was fighting over vast territories against a British army 3,000 miles from home. Many times in the following six years the American army was nearly defeated by the superior training and numbers of the British troops, but gradually the tide turned. As the war continued, France and Spain sent help, declaring war on Britain.

On July 4, 1776, Congress, the American parliament, drew up the formal Declaration of Independence in Philadelphia. This stated that America would no longer obey the British government and that the United States would be an independent republic.

In 1781 at Yorktown in Virginia, the British forces were forced to surrender to a combined American and French army, and it became clear that the United States had won. For a time George III and the British government refused to accept defeat. But at the Treaty of Versailles in 1783 the independence of the colonies was recognized and peace was made between Britain, America, France and Spain. The war was over and the United States had gained her independence.

This is the first draft of the Declaration of Independence in Jefferson's own handwriting, with his corrections.

WHERE did the Light Brigade charge?
WHERE was Napoleon banished to after Waterloo?

THE LIGHT BRIGADE

The famous Charge of the Light Brigade took place eight miles south of the great port of Sebastopol on the west coast of the Crimean peninsula, near the small harbour of Balaclava. During the Crimean War (1854-56), when the forces of France, Britain and Turkey fought the Russian Army, Balaclava was the Allied base. It was defended by lines of earthworks on the hills around the harbour.

On October 25, 1854, Russian forces attempted to break these lines. Over-running some Turks on the heights and seizing their guns, the Russians then descended to the plains and attacked the British forces. The British Heavy Brigade drove them back over a low ridge of hills crossing the plain.

Then occured one of the most famous feats in the chronicles of the British Army, the Charge of the Light Brigade. Led by Lord Cardigan, 673 horsemen rode up a valley under heavy Russian fire. They charged a mile and a half up the valley to capture some Russian guns. They achieved their objective, but only 195 men returned. Among them was Lord Cardigan, who behaved as if the charge had been of no special significance.

Boarding his yacht, where he was living during the campaign, he bathed, dined and went to bed.

This most gallant action would have never taken place if a mistake had not been made in the giving of orders by the High Command. The 673 men of the Light Brigade had charged straight at the wrong guns!

Alfred, Lord Tennyson, a famous Victorian poet, immortalized the charge of the Brigade in the poem he wrote to celebrate it.

NAPOLEON'S EXILE

On July 15, 1815, after his defeat at Waterloo, Napoleon surrendered to the British and was exiled to the remote island of St Helena in the South Atlantic, 1,200 miles off the African coast.

The actual surrender was made to Captain Maitland of the British frigate Bellerophon. Napoleon was transferred to the Northumberland and then taken to St Helena.

This island is only $10\frac{1}{2}$ miles long and $6\frac{1}{2}$ miles wide. Napoleon had no force at his disposal, as he did on the Mediterranean island of Elba, where he was given sovereignty during his first exile.

He was to spend six years on the island before his death. He frequently quarrelled with Sir Hudson Lowe, the Governor, who was very conscientious at thwarting all Napoleon's hopes of escape. He never gave up these attempts, but he also found time to write his memoirs.

He died on May 5, 1821. There were rumours that he had been poisoned, but modern historians and doctors believe it is far more likely that he had cancer of the stomach.

THE KLONDIKE

The Klondike was—and still is—in remote north-western Canada on the borders of Alaska. This area is now part of the Yukon Territory. Dawson, once the capital of the Klondike, lies on the bank of the Yukon river.

For a time Dawson was a bustling town of 10,000 people. Now the population has dwindled to less than 1,000. But there is much less gold than there was at the beginning of the century, and it was only the promise of gold that persuaded people to live so far north in such frozen wastes. For in the streams and creeks of the area the gravel was rich in gold.

At the peak of the Gold Rush in the Klondike more than 30,000 newcomers arrived in four years. In 1900 gold worth more than $22 million was found in the region. Only six years later little more than $5 million in gold was found. By 1910 most of the people had left. A few had made fortunes but the rest were simply cold and disappointed.

Gold production still continues there. But since the remaining gold is underground and almost all the ground is frozen, mining is today a most expensive and very difficult operation. The glorious days of the Klondike are only a memory.

WHERE do the stars and stripes come from?   WHERE did
WHERE did the Dalai Lama live?

Delaware	Dec. 7, 1787	Michigan	Jan. 26, 1837
Pennsylvania	Dec. 12, 1787	Florida	Mar. 3, 1845
New Jersey	Dec. 18, 1787	Texas	Dec. 29, 1845
Georgia	Jan. 2, 1788	Iowa	Dec. 28, 1846
Connecticut	Jan. 9, 1788	Wisconsin	May 29, 1848
Massachusetts	Feb. 6, 1788	California	Sept. 9, 1850
Maryland	Apr. 28, 1788	Minnesota	May 11, 1858
South Carolina	May 23, 1788	Oregon	Feb. 14, 1859
New Hampshire	June 21, 1788	Kansas	Jan. 29, 1861
Virginia	June 25, 1788	West Virginia	June 20, 1863
New York	July 26, 1788	Nevada	Oct. 31, 1864
North Carolina	Nov. 21, 1789	Nebraska	Mar. 1, 1867
Rhode Island	May 29, 1790	Colorado	Aug. 1, 1876
Vermont	Mar. 4, 1791	North Dakota	Nov. 2, 1889
Kentucky	June 1, 1792	South Dakota	Nov. 2, 1889
Tennessee	June 1, 1796	Montana	Nov. 8, 1889
Ohio	Mar. 1, 1803	Washington	Nov. 11, 1889
Louisiana	Apr. 30, 1812	Idaho	July 3, 1890
Indiana	Dec. 11, 1816	Wyoming	July 10, 1890
Mississippi	Dec. 10, 1817	Utah	Jan. 4, 1896
Illinois	Dec. 3, 1818	Oklahoma	Nov. 16, 1907
Alabama	Dec. 14, 1819	New Mexico	Jan. 6, 1912
Maine	Mar. 15, 1820	Arizona	Feb. 14, 1912
Missouri	Aug. 10, 1821	Alaska	Jan. 3, 1959
Arkansas	June 15, 1836	Hawaii	Aug. 21, 1959

STARS & STRIPES

In the early days of the American War of Independence each state adopted a flag of its own. South Carolina had a flag of red and blue stripes adorned with rattlesnakes. That of Massachusetts bore a pine tree. Even the colours carried by different regiments differed according to the taste of their commanders. This was confusing, especially at sea, where one ship might well end up firing on her own ally!

The Rhodes Island flag was the first to contain any stars. There were 13 stars representing the 13 colonies which later were to become the first members of the United States.

In 1776 Washington's new continental army displayed its flag. This time there were no stars. Still in the top left-hand corner was the British Grand Union flag, with its crosses of St George and St Andrew—a sign, one supposes, that independence was not yet the Americans' intention. But around the British emblem appeared the stripes: six white horizontal stripes and seven red ones, again giving the total of 13.

It was not until 1777, almost a year after the adoption of the Declaration of Independence, that Congress adopted a design for the national flag. This consisted of 13 stars (in place of the Grand Union flag) and 13 stripes, alternately red and white.

Every time a new state was accepted in the Union a new star and a new stripe would be added to the flag. By 1795 the flag was getting a little cramped; there was no room for any more stripes. So Congress decided that the flag should contain only 13 stripes representing the original states, and that a star for each new state should be added on the July 4 following its admission to the Union.

In 1959 Alaska became the 49th state and in the same year Hawaii became the 50th and most recent.

ady Godiva ride naked through the town?

WHERE is Golgotha?

LADY GODIVA

Since 1678 Lady Godiva's legendary ride naked through the streets of Coventry, England, has been reenacted every seven or eight years. But today the lady wears a body stocking. The famous ride, if it took place, happened around the year 1057, according to the chronicler Roger of Wendover (d. 1236). Godiva, her long hair falling loosely round her body, rode through the market place accompanied by two soldiers.

Legend has it that Lady Godiva pleaded with Leofric, Earl of Mercia, to lessen the townspeople's tax burden. Exasperated, the earl declared he would do as she asked, if she rode naked through the town. Lady Godiva did so and the earl cut the townspeople's taxes. Over the years the legend became embellished. The soldiers disappeared and, in the 17th Century, the legend of Peeping Tom crept into the story. Tom is said to have been struck blind because he could not resist peeping at Lady Godiva through a window as she rode by.

The true facts record that Coventry's early fame rested on the foundation of a Benedictine monastery by Leofric and his wife Godgifu (the real name of Godiva) in 1043.

The phrase "to send to Coventry" (to refuse to speak with someone) might well have been the fate of Peeping Tom. But although the origin of the phrase is uncertain it seems more likely to have originated during the Civil War. Captured supporters of King Charles were sent by Cromwell's forces to Coventry for imprisonment.

THE DALAI LAMA

The first Dalai Lama, head of an order of Buddhist Monks in Tibet, lived in the Tashilhumpo monastery, which he founded. He died in 1474, and was called Dge-'dun-grub-pa.

Since then, there have been many Dalai Lamas. Most of them have had both political and religious power. The fifth Dalai Lama moved his residence to Lhasa, where he had an enormous palace built, called the Potala. From there Tibet was governed by him and his descendants.

In 1959, the Dalai Lama had to flee to India, because he was thrown out of Tibet by the Chinese Communists.

GOLGOTHA

Golgotha is just outside the walls of the old city of Jerusalem in Israel. It is named in the New Testament as the place where Jesus was crucified.

Jesus was brought before the Roman governor of the province, Pontius Pilate, and accused of blasphemy. Pilate could find nothing to support the charge and offered to release Jesus. But the chief priests and elders persuaded the people to demand his death. Jesus was beaten by the Roman soldiers, dressed in a scarlet cloak and crowned with thorns to mock him as "King of the Jews", Afterwards he was forced to carry his own cross through the streets of Jerusalem to Golgotha.

The name Golgotha, meaning the place of a skull, is derived from the Aramaic language spoken in that part of Palestine. The word Calvary comes from "calvaria", which is the Latin translation of Golgotha. No one knows why Golgotha was so called, but a very ancient story says that Adam's skull was buried there.

This beautiful 15th Century mural was painted by Philip Goul.

MONTEZUMA

Montezuma was an emperor of the 16th Century ruling over the Aztec empire from one of the greatest capitals in the world at that time—Tenochtitlan in what is now Mexico.

"It was like an enchantment . . . on account of the great towers and temples rising from the water . . . things never heard of, nor seen, nor even dreamed". So wrote the Spanish chronicler Bernal Diaz of the city of some 200,000 people. Montezuma's capital was on an island in Lake Texcoco which had been enlarged by a system of drainage canals, and was joined to the shore by causeways.

Across these causeways Hermán Cortés in 1519 led a force of 400 Spaniards, to be greeted by Montezuma as a god. The Spaniards were shown over the shrine-topped pyramids where human sacrifices were made to the Aztecs' stern war god, Huitzilopochtli.

"The figure . . . had a very broad face and monstrous and terrible eyes, and the whole of his body was covered with precious stones, and gold and pearls . . . There were some braziers and in them were burning the hearts of three Indians they had sacrificed that day." Diaz wrote, describing the scene he witnessed with Cortés. The Aztecs held the Spaniards in awe, but suspicion took over and they realized that Cortés was no god. In this atmosphere, Cortés took Montezuma as a hostage. Hostilities flared, and Montezuma was injured and died.

In the Noche Triste or Night of Sadness which followed, the Spaniards were all but annihilated by the Aztecs. Cortés and some of his men escaped. A year later they captured Tenochtitlan and razed it to the ground. The Spaniards built a town upon the ruins. It is still the capital of a nation—Mexico City.

IRON BATTLESHIPS

The first battle involving "ironclads" was between the Monitor and the Merrimack in March, 1862.

The Monitor was built by the Federals in the North during the Civil War. She had a displacement of only 987 tons. Meanwhile, the Confederates in the South also built an ironclad, the C.S.S. Virginia, better known by her former name Merrimack. She had been a wooden frigate, but was burned down to the waterline by enemy action and rebuilt as an ironclad, sheathed in two inches of metal. Her displacement was 4,636 tons.

In 1862 the ships of the North were maintaining a blockade to prevent supplies reaching the South and the opposing vessels met in battle at Hampton Roads off the south-east coast of Virginia. Thousands of people lined the shores to watch the fight as the ships passed on opposite courses, turned and passed again.

Both crews lacked training and their shooting was ineffective. The Merrimack had more guns, but was heavy and slow. The Monitor was lightly armed, but much faster. The battle was indecisive—the Monitor sheered off and the Merrimack returned to the navy yard.

On the previous day the Merrimack had achieved spectacular success by ramming and sinking the sailing sloop Cumberland and then destroying the Federal sailing frigate Congress by gunfire. Her prowess convinced the public that the day of the wooden man-of-war was ended.

The first ironclad, or armoured warship, had been completed in France in 1858. Next year the British Admiralty ordered two ironclads, the Warrior and the Black Prince. Completed in October 1861 and September 1862 respectively, they each displaced 9,210 tons, could attain a speed of 14 knots and had a complement of 707 offficers and men. These two ships, with the French Gloire and Couronne, were the first battleships, although the name was not then applied to them.

The Monitor, with its round turret, is in the foreground.

ron battleships fight? **WHERE** did Columbus land?

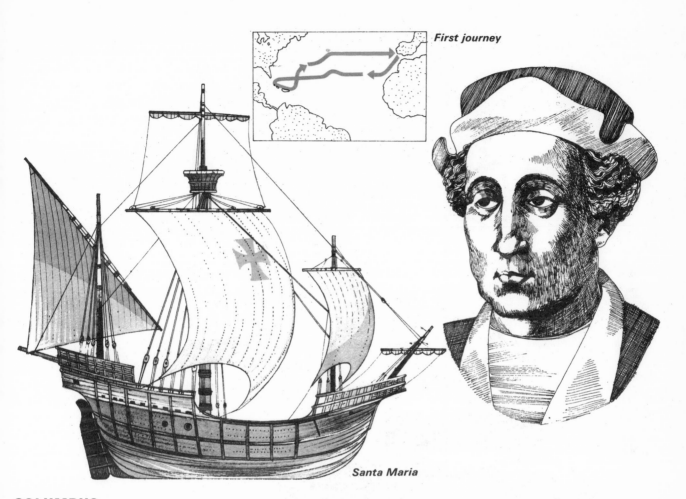

First journey

Santa Maria

COLUMBUS

Christopher Columbus, on his famous voyage of 1492, made landfall after nine weeks at sea on an island he named San Salvador — now also known as Watling Island — in the Bahamas.

Columbus, a Genoese, set sail with three ships, the Santa Maria, the Pinta and the Nina, under the patronage of King Ferdinand and Queen Isabella of Spain. This voyage was the first of his attempts to find a sea route to Asia.

After leaving San Salvador, Columbus discovered the island of Cuba and then Haiti, where he left some members of his crews garrisoning a fort called La Navidad. His flagship had been wrecked and there was not enough room on the remaining two ships to take all the men home.

Believing that he had reached Asia, Columbus returned to Spain where he was given a great reception. He came back with some "Indians" to show at court and evidence of the existence of gold in the New World.

On his second voyage Columbus founded the city of Isabella on Haiti. Calling at La Navidad he found that his "colony" had been killed by the natives. The Spaniards had treated them with such cruelty, it seems, that the formerly mild-natured people had sought revenge. Columbus pushed on westwards and explored more of the Caribbean Sea, although he still believed Cuba to be the mainland of Asia. He returned to Isabella, but increasing difficulties and trouble with his own subordinates exhausted him, and he was ill for many months.

The Spanish general Ojeda and Columbus's brother, Bartholomew, were responsible for the crushing of a so-called rebellion of the natives, and in 1495 five ship-loads of captured men were sent to Spain as slaves. Eventually Columbus fell from favour at the Spanish court. Although he was fitted out for another voyage during which he discovered Trinidad, the king and queen sent out a new governor to the new territories.

This man, Bobadilla, became so infuriated with the behaviour of Columbus and his brother that he sent them back to Spain in irons. Insisting on wearing these irons in the presence of Ferdinand and Isabella, Columbus was forgiven.

On his last voyage in 1502, Columbus reached Honduras. After much hardship, he returned to Spain in 1504 and died in 1506, an impoverished and broken man.

WHERE is Tutankhamun's tomb?
WHERE is Wounded Knee? **WHERE** is

WOUNDED KNEE

Wounded Knee is a narrow creek in north-western South Dakota in the United States. One night in 1890 some 400 Sioux Indians, led by Big Foot, camped in a hollow near the creek. The Sioux were on their way back to the reservation after a "ghost dance" ceremony, farther south in the Badlands.

In the morning the Seventh Cavalry lined up their Hotchkiss guns on the hill and the troopers took up positions round the Indian camp.

The Indians were ordered to hand over their weapons. Suspicious and fearful, they refused. In the subsequent search a shot was fired. At once the machine guns opened up, and in a short time most of the Indians were dead. Survivors, including women and children, were pursued up the creek and gunned down. Heavy snow began to fall, and the bodies were left to freeze grotesquely where they lay. Several days later the dead were heaped on wagons and thrown into a mass grave.

The Seventh Cavalry were awarded 26 Congressional Medals of Honour for their part in the action. The Battle of Wounded Knee, or, more accurately, the Massacre of the Big Foot Band, was the last battle to be fought in America's longest undeclared war.

TUTANKHAMUN

Tutankhamun's tomb is in Egypt, in a place called the Valley of the Kings. Tutankhamun was a pharaoh, who died in 1352 B.C. His name was familiar only to scholars until his tomb was discovered in 1922 by Howard Carter. The tomb was filled with precious jewels, ornaments, vases, furniture, clothes, ornamented coffins, chariots, and the mummified body of the young king himself, wearing a gold mask.

When the Egyptians buried a pharaoh, they took trouble to surround him with beautiful and useful things. They did not believe he was really dead. They thought he would go on living if he were provided with enough things to protect him in his journey through the underworlds, and afterwards.

Most of the kings' tombs were robbed, frequently by local people, of their jewels and gold.

There are several chambers in the tomb—the Antechamber, the Burial Chamber, the Treasury, and the Store Room. In the Antechamber was a beautiful alabaster wishing-cup and a painted wooden casket with brilliant designs. At the doorway of the Treasury was a figure of a God called Anubis, a sort of jackal-like dog, who was supposed to keep watch over the dead. Round his neck he wore a scarf decorated with lotus and cornflowers.

William Penn buried? WHERE was Custer's last stand?

WILLIAM PENN

William Penn (1644-1718), who gave his name to the state of Pennsylvania in the United States, is buried in the graveyard of an early Quaker meeting house in Jordans, in the English county of Buckinghamshire.

He was the son of Admiral Sir William Penn (1621-70) and became a convert to Quakerism in 1661. These peaceful people were persecuted and despised. William Penn was expelled from Oxford University because he joined the sect, and was later imprisoned in the Tower of London.

In 1681 Charles II granted Penn a domain of some 50,000 square miles of English Crown land in America in payment of a debt owed by the Crown to his father. Persecuted in England, the Quakers were not allowed to enter any of the established American colonies. To found a haven for people of all religions, and in the hope of converting the warlike Red Indians, Penn sent out the first settlers to his newly-aquired colony which he named Pennsylvania (Penn's forestland). He, too, went out a year later.

He gave the settlers democratic government and made friends with the Delaware Indians who agreed to "live in love with William Penn and his children as long as the sun and moon gave light". Penn lived at Philadelphia, the capital of his colony, but after two years was called back to England on business and was absent for 15 years.

After a period of trouble he revisited Pennsylvania in 1899 and granted a charter to its 20,000 inhabitants which remained in force for 75 years until the American War of Independence.

In 1701 Penn returned to England to find that his unscrupulous steward had robbed him of his fortune. He was imprisoned for debt and the conditions of the jail affected his health. His friends secured his release, and he lived quietly until his death on May 30, 1718. The fine old building in whose graveyard he is buried has been preserved and is open to the public.

"GENERAL" CUSTER

"General" Custer made his famous last stand on the banks of the Little Big Horn river near what is now the interchange for United States Highways 87 and 212, in the State of Montana. Today the Custer Battlefield National Monument marks the scene of the battle.

George Armstrong Custer, born in 1839, was called "General" by the men of the 7th Cavalry Brigade under his command. He had shown his brilliance as a cavalry officer in the American Civil War (1861-65) reaching the rank of major-general.

In 1876 when Sioux and Cheyennes were on the warpath with Chief Sitting Bull as their leader, Custer and his 7th Cavalry Brigade were under the command of General Terry. The brigade of 655 men was ordered by Terry to advance towards the Indians, but not to attack until the rest of the army—composed of three columns under General Crook, Gibbon and Terry—had moved into position.

Custer reached the Little Big Horn to see the large Indian camp on the opposite side of the river. For a reason that will never be known, Custer decided to disobey orders and attack. Dividing his brigade into three, he sent Major Reno and Captain Benteen, each with three companies, to attack the flanks. At the same time he led 264 troopers on a frontal approach across the river.

His force stood no chance when the Indians attacked. The troopers dismounted from their horses to seek cover, but there was none. When the Indians drove off their horses, the troopers' fate was sealed.

Believing that Reno and Benteen would soon come to their aid, they fought bravely, but the flank attacks had been foiled and the cavalry put to flight. Custer and 264 men fought to the last man.

WHERE was Nelson born?   WHERE were the remains of

NELSON'S BIRTHPLACE

The great British naval hero, Horatio Nelson, who defeated the French at Trafalgar in 1805 in one of the most memorable of all sea battles, was born at Burnham Thorpe in Norfolk, England. His father was rector of that parish. Horatio's mother (née Suckling) was related to Sir Robert Walpole the British statesman and Prime Minister.

Nelson's uncle, Captain Maurice Suckling, who later became Comptroller of the Navy, gave Horatio his first taste of the sea. Horatio, who was educated in his home county of Norfolk by the North Sea, was entered in the ship Raisonnable by Captain Suckling in 1770 when there was an alarm of war with Spain. But the dispute with Spain was quickly settled, and Nelson was packed off in a merchant vessel to the West Indies to gain experience.

This was the beginning of a hard apprenticeship during which time Nelson visited such remote areas as the Arctic and the East Indies.

Five years after his first appointment at sea Nelson fell ill and was invalided home. It was not until two years later, having just passed his examination as lieutenant, that his remarkable career began in earnest.

NOAH'S ARK

After seven months afloat Noah came to rest, the Bible tells us, "upon the mountains of Ararat". Mount Ararat, an extinct volcanic massif 17,160 feet high consists of two peaks seven miles apart and separated by a saddle 8,800 feet above sea level. It stands in Turkish territory overlooking the point where the frontiers of Turkey, Iran and Soviet Armenia converge, and is about 25 miles in diameter.

The story of the Ark is still a living tradition among the Armen-ians, who believe themselves to be the first race of men to appear in the world after the Deluge. Local legend maintains that the remains of the Ark were long to be seen on top of the mountain. Near the foot of a mountain chasm stood the village of Aghuri, where, according to tradition, Noah built his altar and made sacrifice after his safe deliverance, and where he planted his vineyard. The village was destroyed by earthquake in 1840. A Persian legend refers to Ararat as the cradle of the human race; the Persian name for it is Koh-i-Nuh, meaning Noah's Mountain.

For centuries the Armenians believed that God forbade anyone to reach the top of Ararat and view the remains of the Ark. However, on September 7, 1829, Johann Hacob von Parrot (1792–1840), a German in the Russian service, made the first successful ascent known. Since then the mountain has been climbed many times. The ascent is said to be not difficult.

Noah's Ark discovered?   WHERE is Dunkirk?
WHERE did Prester John live?

DUNKIRK

Dunkirk is a seaport of Northern France lying between Calais and the Belgian coast, but for millions of people all over the world Dunkirk is one of the most evocative names of the Second World War. For it was from Dunkirk and its 10-mile stretch of beaches that the British evacuated some 338,200 soldiers after the collapse of Belgium and immediately before the collapse of France. Today, Dunkirk has become another name for the supreme heroism that can snatch a victory from defeat.

The troop evacuation took place between May 26 and June 3, 1940. The men were under constant German bombardment both from the land and from the air. At home in England, the British organized an immortal flotilla of small boats. Thames pleasure boats, cabin-cruisers, fishing smacks, even rowing boats were pressed into service —all, of course, on a volunteer basis. The "little ships" ferried the troops from the beaches to the waiting Navy ships.

Evacuation first began from the damaged harbour at Dunkirk, but by May 28 heavy German bombing had severely restricted the harbour's usefulness. By the end of June 1 the greater part of the British Expeditionary Force had been removed, although rescue operations continued until June 4.

The toll of ships was considerable. Out of 41 destroyers used by the British, 6 were sunk and 19 damaged. Most of the expeditionary force's supplies and materials were lost. The British were reduced to their weakest point. But Dunkirk was the great turning point in the war. Hitler's Germany had, it seemed, reached its greatest point of menace, and was never to seem so threatening again.

PRESTER JOHN

Nobody knows for certain and, indeed, nobody has ever succeeded in proving that Prester John ever lived. The legend of Prester John or John the Priest—Prester is a shortened form of Presbyter—dates from the Middle Ages. According to these early legends Prester John was a mighty Christian potentate, a sort of King Priest of the Indies, of fabulous wealth and power.

In the year 1165, the story goes, a letter was sent by Prester John, King of the Indies, to various European rulers, in which he claimed to be a "lord of lords" and hinted that he enjoyed a divine authority.

The land of John was apparently an earthly paradise flowing with milk and honey. Justice and peace ruled supreme. Envy, flattery, greed, theft—none of these evils existed in John's kingdom. Poverty, too, did not exist. So many people enjoyed high-sounding titles at John's court, the letter claimed, that John himself used the plain title of Presbyter or Priest. Apparently John's butler, in this fabled kingdom, was an archbishop and even his cook was a king.

The idea behind this alleged letter to the European princes was that they should feel humbled that one as mighty as John should use such a modest title. Really the letter was an ingenious forgery and a satire on the princes of Europe.

But the fable of a great Christian ruler lingered on. The crusaders loved the idea of this powerful Christian monarch ruling in the mysterious East. So the territories of Prester John were duly shown on medieval maps, although the boundaries were always vague.

In later centuries it was suggested that the land of John really lay in Ethiopia, and gradually this became the accepted version of the legend. Robert Louis Stevenson makes use of the story in his adventure novel, *Prester John*.

WHERE did Robin Hood live?　WHERE is Pompeii?

ROBIN HOOD

Robin Hood lived in Sherwood Forest, near Nottingham in the centre of England. In those 12th Century days a vast region of open tracts, woodland glades and great oaks used to stretch for many miles from the city northwards. This region was called Sherwood Forest.

Until the time of the Normans the forest was used for hunting by the people of that region, or shire, and thereby acquired its earlier name of Shire Wood. The common people's right to hunt ceased when the Norman kings took over the forest for their own use. Strict laws were passed and special courts were set up to preserve them.

Whether Robin Hood and his merry band of followers, which included Little John, Friar Tuck, Will Scarlet and Maid Marian, ever exsisted is difficult to establish.

Certainly by the end of the 12th Century, with control of royal Sherwood in the hands of feudal barons, the common people deeply resented the harsh and oppressive rule under which they lived. The time was ripe for stories about a man who robbed the rich to feed the poor.

The character of Robin Hood represented the ideals of the common people of the late Middle Ages. Ballads about his exploits have been preserved and may date from the 14th and 15th Centuries. In 1795 Joseph Ritson first published a collection of these in book form.

Over the years stories of the carefree folk-hero and his band of happy followers, living an idyllic life in the woodland glades of Sherwood during the days of the Plantagenet kings, have become the subject of many books.

POMPEII

For nearly 1,700 years Pompeii in southern Italy was a dead and buried city, forgotten by all except historians. But for more than 600 years before disaster overtook it, Pompeii was a proud city and port of the Roman Empire in the shadow of Mount Vesuvius on the Bay of Naples.

On the morning of August 24, in the year A.D. 79 an event occured that was to preserve for us the story of Roman everyday life. Sixteen years previously an earthquake had damaged Pompeii, a city where wealthy Romans had their country villas, and the damage had been repaired. Now, Vesuvius once again erupted violently. For three days the sky was darkened, and a deadly hail of volcanic ash and pumice rained down upon the doomed city.

By the time the eruption settled down, Pompeii lay under a blanket of pumice eight to ten feet thick. The outlines of the land had been so altered that the sea was now nearly two miles away. Two thousand of the city's 20,000 inhabitants died in the disaster, suffocated by the sulphurous fumes or crushed by falling roofs. Pompeii, it seemed, had been wiped off the face of the earth.

So it was until, in 1748, a peasant digging in his vineyard unearthed some statues. This led to a remarkable record of a Roman city in its heyday being brought to light.

Excavation has revealed rows of shops and houses, the forum or market-place, with temples adjoining business houses, an open air theatre, and public baths. In the museum at Naples are many thousands of objects recovered from Pompeii—statues and paintings, pens and ink-bottles, coins, looking-glasses and even charred food served on the day of the eruption nearly 1,900 years ago.

This statue of Robin Hood is at Nottingham.

WHERE do Mormons live? WHERE did Mohammed live?

A view of the excavated Roman city of Pompeii.

THE MORMONS

Most Mormons live in the state of Utah in the United States. There are Mormons elsewhere in the world, but Utah has been their chief home since 1846, when a picked company of 150 Mormons under their leader Brigham Young, came to the valley of the Great Salt Lake in the Rocky Mountains with their horses and livestock, their covered wagons filled with provisions, implements and seed grain.

Sixteen years earlier the Church of Jesus Christ of Latter-Day Saints had been founded by Joseph Smith (1805-44) at Fayette in New York State. Joseph Smith claimed to have obtained the Book of Mormon, through a number of revelations, in 1827. This book is regarded by followers of the sect as of equal authority with the Old and New Testaments.

In spite of persecution, the Mormons increased in numbers and sent missionaries to European countries. Converts were encouraged to emigrate to the United States and to join the "Gathering of Israel". Persecution in America increased and the Mormons were driven from one state to another.

Joseph Smith and other leaders were arrested in 1844, and he and his brother were murdered in the jail at Carthage, Missouri. The leadership passed to Brigham Young, and the Mormons left Missouri for Illinois.

When in 1846 the Mormons were expelled from Illinois, they decided to move beyond the frontier of the United States, at that time the Missouri River, and settle in undeveloped land in the far west where no one would molest them. So it was that Brigham Young, now recognized as one of the great pioneers of American history, led the Mormons on their trek across the great plains. It was mostly desert country in the valley of the Great Salt Lake, but, joined by bigger parties, the Mormons succeeded by tremendous effort in turning it into a fertile land.

Churches and schools were built and industries started. So successful were the Mormons in establishing a thriving community that, after only four years, the Territory of Utah was recognized by the Government and Young was appointed its first governor.

MOHAMMED

The Prophet Mohammed lived most of the time in Mecca, where he was born in A.D. 570. The holy city of Mecca is situated in what is now Saudi Arabia. It is the greatest place of pilgrimage for members of the Mohammedan religion which the Prophet founded. Hundreds of thousands of Mohammedans make the sacred journey to Mecca every year.

After his father's death, Mohammed was a poor shepherd boy in the mountains near Mecca. As he grew older he often used to go alone into the mountains to pray. He did not begin preaching until he was 40, a few years after he thought he heard the archangel Gabriel speaking to him on Mount Hira.

Mohammed taught simply that there was one all-powerful God, and that men should try to serve him through prayer, helping one another and trying to lead a good life.

In 622, persecution from men, who disagreed with his teaching, led to the flight or "hegira" of Mohammed from Mecca to the neighbouring city of Medina. This is the year from which the whole Mohammedan world reckons time. In Medina, Mohammed developed a more formal and organized religion. But he wanted Mecca to become the chief centre for Mohammedans. Already they faced Mecca when they prayed, because they believed it was a holy place.

In 630, the Mohammedans advanced on Mecca, and took the city easily. The people who lived there then accepted the Mohammedan religion which today has hundreds of millions of followers throughout the world, especially in Africa, Asia and eastern Europe.

It is now one of the most influential and widespread religious systems in the world.

WHERE did General Lee surrender to General Grant?
WHERE was the Mutiny on the Bounty?

LEE'S SURRENDER

General Lee and his poorly equipped, outnumbered Confederate Army surrendered to General Ulysses S. Grant, commander of the Federal Army, on April 9, 1865 at the court house of the Virginian town of Appomattox.

"The very best soldier I ever saw in the field," said an American general of Robert E. Lee, shortly before Lee resigned his commission in the United States Army.

Lee had been offered the command of the Federal (Northern) Army by President Lincoln. But because he was a Southerner, born in the state of Virginia, he chose to fight on the opposite side.

This defeat by the North in the American Civil War (1861-65) was a bitter pill to take.

The Battle of Gettysburg in July, 1863, was the decisive turning point in the fortunes of General Lee and the Confederates. Before this most bloody battle, Lee had many victories. Among them were Cedar Run and Bull Run, and the outstanding triumph of Chancellorsville in May, 1863. Lee wanted to build on these achievements and carry the war to the North. Success there might have led to the seizure of the rich farmlands and industrial centres of Pennsylvania for the refurbishing of his

much depleted supplies, and eventually a negotiated settlement. But the victory at Gettysburg by the Federals under General George G. Meade meant that Lee failed to get his supplies.

In the spring of 1864, General Grant, now in command of the Federals, took the field in person against Lee. In the following spring he compelled the Confederate general to abandon Virginia's capital, Richmond, and chased him westward to defeat.

Lee died in 1870, Grant went on to be the 18th President. The court house at Appomattox is now preserved in a national park.

WHERE did David kill Goliath?
WHERE did the Queen of Sheba live?

DAVID AND GOLIATH

The famous fight in which the boy David slew the giant Goliath took place about 15 miles south-west of Jerusalem, in the Valley of Elah in Israel.

David was the youngest of eight brothers and looked after his father's sheep at Bethlehem while the Israelites under King Saul were at war with the Philistines. The First Book of Samuel in the Bible tells how David was sent by his father to take food to the Israelites' camp. Goliath had challenged the Israelites to send a man to do battle with him, the result to decide which array should have the fruits of victory.

No Israelite had dared to take up the challenge. But David persuaded Saul to let him fight Goliath, saying the giant was no more dangerous an adversary than the lion and bear he had slain while protecting his father's sheep.

The two contestants rushed to meet each other, the giant in full armour with sword, spear and shield, the boy with only a sling and five smooth stones from the river. David took a stone in his sling and aimed it at Goliath. The giant was hit on the forehead and stunned. David then killed him with his own sword. The Philistines fled, pursued by the victorious Israelites.

MUTINY ON THE BOUNTY

The famous Mutiny on the Bounty took place on a voyage to the South Seas. In 1787 Captain William Bligh (1754-1817) set sail in the British naval transport ship Bounty with a crew of 44 men for the island of Tahiti in the Pacific Ocean.

The Bounty was a small ship even by the standards of the second half of the 18th Century, displacing 250 tons and only 90 feet long.

Bligh's task was to collect cuttings of bread-fruit trees from the beautiful South Sea island, only recently discovered by Captain Cook, and carry them to the West Indies. There it was hoped the cuttings might thrive and provide food for the African slaves on the sugar plantations.

Captain Bligh was a stern disciplinarian and a bad-tempered man. His temper did not lessen the general discomfort of the voyage to Tahiti. The crew, staying for several months on the lovely island while the cuttings were being gathered, enjoyed the contrast to their cramped quarters and the ill-tempered captain.

So not long after the Bounty had set sail for the West Indies some of the crew demonstrated their renewed discontent. On April 28, 1789 Fletcher Christian, the master's mate, took control of the ship by force. The captain and those men loyal to him were put in a 23-foot open boat. With no chart and few provisions, Bligh and 18 men sailed 3,618 miles in seven weeks to the island of Timor. Whatever his faults, Bligh proved his seamanship. On reaching England, he reported the mutiny.

Christian and the mutineers returned with the Bounty to Tahiti where some of the men decided to settle. But Christian thought it best to move on and sailed to the remote Pacific island of Pitcairn with seven of the mutineers, their Tahitian wives and some male islanders. Some of their descendents still live on the island today.

The men who had elected to remain on Tahiti were later captured and returned to England for trial. Three were hanged. Captain Bligh continued to serve in the navy and eventually rose to the rank of vice-admiral.

QUEEN OF SHEBA

There is a legend in Ethiopia that her emperors are descended from the Queen of Sheba and Solomon, King of Israel, who died about 937 B.C. The story relates that Aksum, the once-splendid city on the high central plateau of Ethiopia, was formerly called Sheba. It is said Queen Makeda of Aksum visited King Solomon at Jerusalem, and that their son, Menelik, became the first Ethiopian emperor.

But Aksum in the time of Solomon was probably not large enough to have a ruler of such wealth and power as the queen of the story. However, there could have been such a Queen of Sheba in the Yemen, the southern part of the Arabian peninsula.

The kingdom of Saba, which may have been the Biblical Sheba, straddled the profitable incense routes that stretched from the Hadhramaut, on Arabia's south coast, to ports on the Mediterranean. It was a rich and powerful kingdom and its inhabitants built a great dam and irrigation system which made the land lush and fertile. Today only a few ruins of the old kingdom survive.

Medicine and the Body

THE METATARSALS

The metatarsal bones are found in your feet. The foot is made up of the tarsus, or ankle, which consists of seven bones; the metatarsus, which consists of five bones, or metatarsals; and the five free digits or toes.

Metatarsals are short and irregularly cube-like in shape. Their surfaces are rough for the attachment of ligaments. In number and general form they are like the similarly positioned bones of the hand, which are known as the metacarpals.

Although the bones of the feet and hand move in a generally similar sort of way there are, of course, important differences. One of the most obvious differences is that in the bones of the hand the thumb has a far greater play of movement than the big toe in the foot. A joint at the base of the thumb allows many more movements than in the case of the big toe.

This "opposable finger and thumb" is one of the physical attributes that has enabled man to reach the peak of the animal "league" table. It is one of the keys to human development.

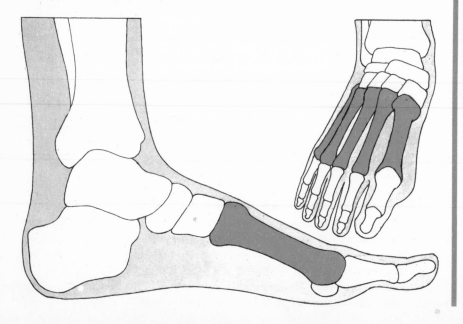

DREAMS

The simple answer is either they are stored in your memory or you forget them. But this question makes us ask a great number of other questions. What is the difference between day-dreaming and the dreams we have when we are asleep? Can dreams foretell the future? How long do they really last? Do we have dreams in

you wake up?

Charles Dickens dreams of the immortal characters in his famous books

colour or only in black and white? Why do we forget some dreams and remember others? Are dreams good for us, or bad? Why do some dreams wake us up at once and others not?

Some experts say that to be healthy in mind, we have to dream every night, whether we remember them or not. There is a book called

An Experiment with Time by J. W. Dunne, which tells us that the author used to note down in the morning the dreams he had in the night, and that sometimes his dreams foretold what was going to happen in the future.

He suggests that when we are wide awake our sense of time is vertical, so that we are aware only

of the present moment, but that when we are asleep, time becomes for us horizontal, so that we can travel into the past and the future. Other experts say that we dream of doing the things which for various reasons, we cannot do in our waking hours. So we try to realize in our sleep wishes that cannot be realized by day.

WHERE is your funny bone? WHERE does the body store WHERE are the Islets of Langerhans?

FUNNY BONE

Your funny bone is in your arm. It is the long, almost straight bone which extends from your shoulder to your elbow. At the top end it is attached to your scapula, or shoulder blade. At the elbow it is attached to the two bones in your lower arm which are called the radius and the ulna, which in turn are attached to your wrist and hand.

The funny bone carries the very strong biceps muscles—the ones which bulge up on the top of your arm when you bend your elbow and bring your hand up to your shoulder. The bone is grooved to carry the nerves to your hand. These nerves convey messages to and from your brain so that you can control your hand and use it to feel things.

Some people think your funny bone is so called because, when you knock a particular part of your elbow, you get a funny, tingling sensation. The real reason is because the medical name for this bone is the humerus—and since it is pronounced "humorous", the description of "funny bone" has now passed into universal use.

THE BODY'S ENERGY

Certain cells of the body store surplus food in the form of fat or animal starch. This is released from storage when there is not enough food in the blood to supply the energy demands of the body.

Few of the things we eat can be used directly by the body cells. They must be changed chemically before they can supply the energy required. This is called digestion and is carried out in the stomach and in the small intestine, from where this digested food must be transported to the cells.

Now the food, in the form of digested sugars, proteins, and starches dissolved in water, passes into the blood system where, as blood, it can circulate through the body in less than one minute. Once the food is in the blood stream it is soon delivered to all the cells of the body by means of the red corpuscles in the blood.

It is when this supply falls low that the energy stores come into action.

ISLETS OF LANGERHANS

These islets are not to be found in an atlas but are located in the human pancreas, which manufactures juices to aid the digestion of fats and continues the work of the saliva and gastric juices.

Langerhans was a German anatomist (1847-88) who gave his name to two other parts of the body. He discovered cells in the epidermis called Langerhans Cells and also the Langerhans Layer which is a layer of the skin.

There are many groups of cells without ducts distributed through the pancreas. But the importance of the Islets of Langerhans is that their beta cells are a source of insulin. It is damage to or removal of the Islets of Langerhans that leads to pancreatic diabetes. Insulin, which is a protein, is synthesized by the beta cells.

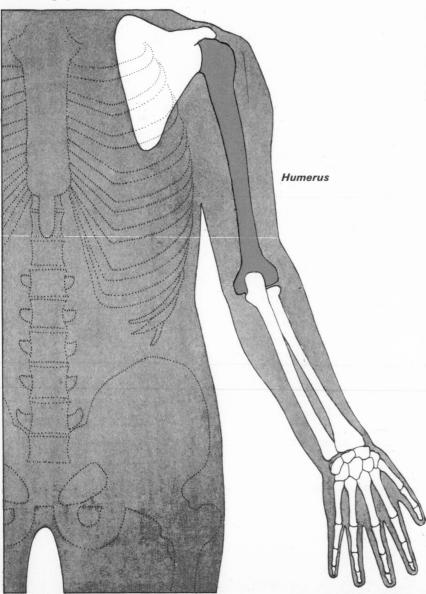

Humerus

its energy?   WHERE do teeth come from?
WHERE are your sweat glands?

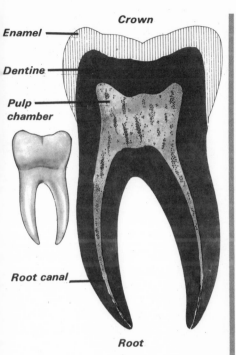

Crown

Enamel

Dentine

Pulp chamber

Root canal

Root

TEETH

Teeth are formed from specialized cells which produce the three parts of the tooth—root, neck, and crown. The outer coating of the crown is made of hard enamel. This covers the dentine which forms most of the bony framework of the teeth. Channels in the dentine contain blood vessels and nerves which make up the innermost part of the tooth, the dental pulp.

Most of the higher animals, including man, are born without teeth. They develop two sets, called the milk teeth and the permanent teeth.

A human mouth contains 32 teeth. Their function is to cut, tear, and grind food, and they are specialized for this. So in each jaw there are four incisors (for biting), two canines (for holding or tearing), four bicuspids (chewing teeth with a cutting edge), and six molars (for grinding).

"Wisdom" teeth, the largest of all, are situated at the back of the jaw, and may not arrive until we are grown up.

SWEAT GLANDS

Sweat glands, of which everybody has approximately two million, are distributed all over the body on the skin surface. They are not, however, distributed evenly. The palms of our hands and the soles of our feet may have as many as 2,500 sweat glands per square inch, whereas on our backs there may be as few as 500 per square inch.

Each gland breaks the skin surface in the form of a sweat pore. These pores are too small to be visible to the naked eye, except on the palms and soles, where there are so many that they just become visible.

In some diseases nerve funtion is lost in certain areas of the body, and these areas also lose the power to sweat. Sweat is a solution of about 99 per cent water with a little sodium chloride (common salt). The body can produce from zero to 2,000 grammes of this substance every hour and even more in strenuous activities.

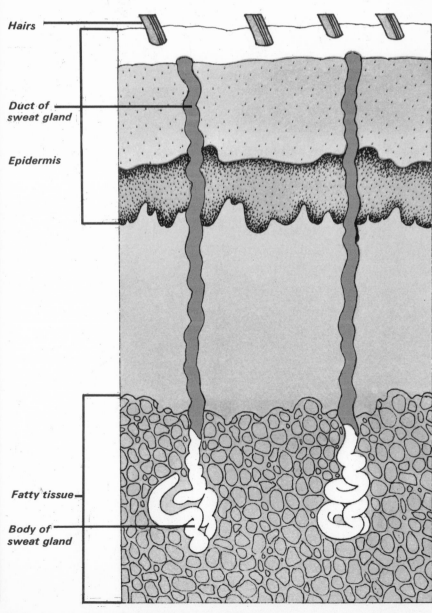

Hairs

Duct of sweat gland

Epidermis

Fatty tissue

Body of sweat gland

WHERE is the aorta?   WHERE would you catch malaria?

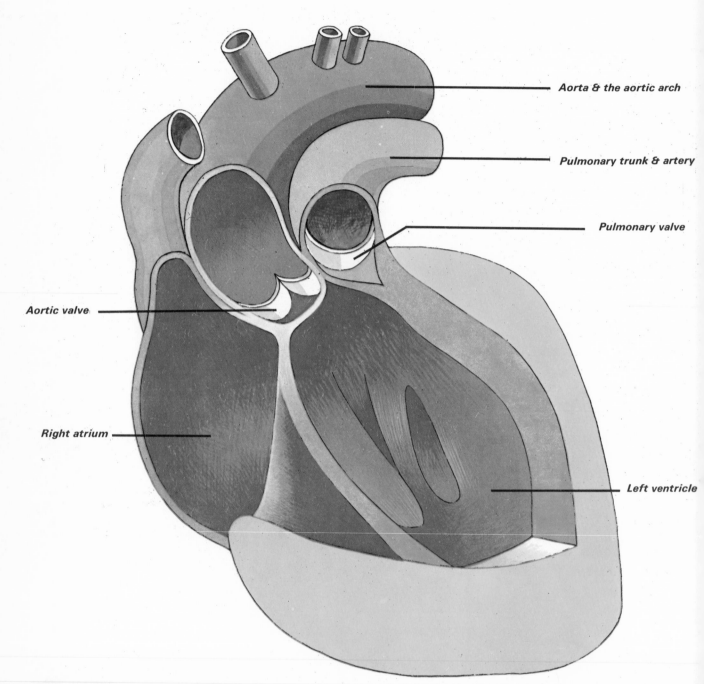

Aorta & the aortic arch

Pulmonary trunk & artery

Pulmonary valve

Aortic valve

Right atrium

Left ventricle

THE AORTA

The aorta is the great artery rising from the left side of the heart, through which the blood passes on its way to all parts of the body except the lungs, which are supplied by another system.

After rising from the heart, the aorta forms an arch, descending down the left side of the body. It passes through the diaphragm into the abdomen, where it divides into two lesser arteries. One of these terminates under the end of the backbone, where man has the vestige of a tail. In animals it continues into the tail as the caudal artery.

The aorta is one of the elastic—or conducting—arteries, which take the blood to the muscular—or distributing—ones, which connect with the veins and smaller blood vessels.

Three valves at the exit of the aorta protect the heart from any back pressure that might develop in the artery and force the blood in the wrong direction.

Inflammation caused by an illness such as rheumatic fever may sometimes cause these valves to leak. This is a serious condition requiring considerable medical care and attention. But in normal cases your aorta will continue to function reliably throughout your life.

WHERE is the cervix?   WHERE are your nerves?

MALARIA

The most likely places to catch malaria would be in tropical and sub-tropical countries, especially in the forested parts of Central and South America, central Africa, Asia, and southern Europe. This is because the female anopheles mosquito, whose bite transmits the disease, breeds in the warm, stagnant, marshy pools found in those parts.

Malaria is said to derive its name from the Italian for "evil air". It causes chills, fever and anaemia, and is sometimes fatal. In India a million people are likely to die from it every year.

The first effective remedy for it, quinine, was used in the 16th Century. It is an infusion from the bark of the cinchona tree. Modern drugs, too, have greatly reduced the threat of malaria. In particular the use of sprays on the mosquitoes' breeding places has been highly effective.

In 1955 the World Health Organization started a mosquito-eradication programme of benefit to nearly 1,200 million people.

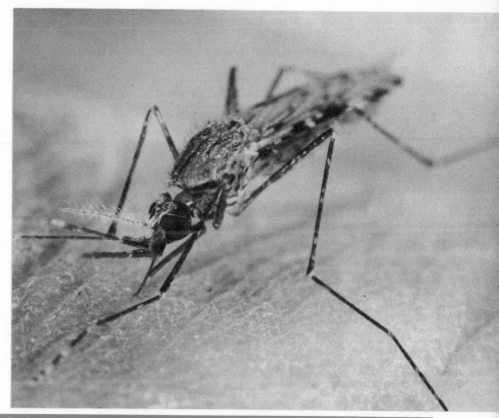

THE CERVIX

The cervix is the name doctors give to the neck of the womb. It is a small opening surrounded by folds of mucous membrane containing mucous-secreting glands. It is supported by two folds of tissue that attach to the backbone.

The first stage of a child's birth occurs when the cervix starts to expand under the influence of rhythmical muscular contractions, until the head can pass through.

The cervix is recognised as a possible cancer site. There is now a service that tests women at regular intervals—three years is usual—for signs of this disease, so that effective early treatment may be started. Scarring or infection following a difficult childbirth may make the cervix more vulnerable.

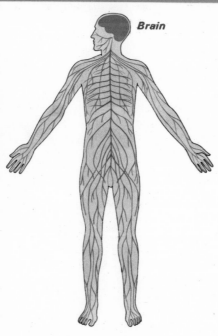

There are so many thousands of nerves spread throughout the body that a drawing cannot possibly show them all. This diagram gives a general idea of their distribution.

THE NERVES

Your nerves are spread all over your body. The organs of the body are composed of tissues. These in turn consist of microscopic units called cells, specialized to perform particular functions such as secretion (glands), contraction (muscles) or conduction (nerves). Likewise the tissues that pick up our nervous system are composed of billions of individual cells located all over the human body. No part of our body is completely insensitive to pain or some other sensation, because nerves are to be found in every part of the human anatomy.

The nervous system is usually considered to have two parts, the peripheral or outside system, which is in direct contact with the things that cause pain or pleasure, and the central system, consisting of the brain and the spinal cord. It is in our central nervous system that all our sensations and reactions are finally registered.

Geography and the Earth

NORTH-WEST PASSAGE

The North-West Passage is a sea route along the north coast of North America between the Atlantic and Pacific oceans. It was first sailed by the Norwegian explorer Roald Amundsen in 1903–1906 in the 47-ton Gjöa.

The search for the Passage started in the 15th Century, when Bristol merchants commissioned the Genoese mariner John Cabot

to find a direct sea route between Britain and the Indies by sailing west. He failed, but discovered the mainland of America on his voyage.

Over the next 350 years, others were to seek the route and many died in the attempt. These brave pioneers included famous characters such as Henry Hudson and Sir Humphrey Gilbert.

In 1845, Sir John Franklin made

his ill-fated voyage. With 129 officers and men in two ships, the Frebus and Terror, Franklin's expedition became icebound in the Victoria Strait. Franklin died and the crew abandoned their vessels and eventually perished.

It was ironic that out of the Royal Navy's efforts to find Franklin came the first successful completion of the North-West Passage, although much of the journey was made on foot. That was in 1854.

The many succeeding voyages included those of the United States nuclear powered submarine Seadragon, which made the first underwater trip in 1960, and of the 1,005 foot S.S. Manhattan, which in 1969 made a voyage from New York to Alaska and back in a little over two months.

But the North-West Passage has never become the great sea route to the East which men dreamed about for so many centuries. Today the Panama Canal provides the only transcontinental sea-link from the West to the East.

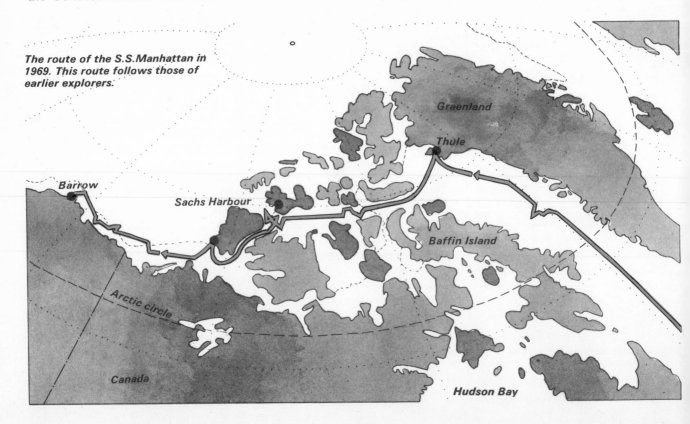

The route of the S.S. Manhattan in 1969. This route follows those of earlier explorers.

Greenland

Thule

Barrow

Sachs Harbour

Baffin Island

Arctic circle

Canada

Hudson Bay

WHERE is the Hellespont? WHERE is the will o' the wisp?

THE HELLESPONT

The Hellespont is the ancient name given to the strait of the Dardanelles which joins the Eastern Mediterranean to the Sea of Marmara. The Sea of Marmara is almost landlocked—except for the Hellespont and the Bosporus which flows into the Black Sea between the Soviet Union and Turkey.

The shores of the Hellespont are formed by the peninsula of Gallipoli in Europe on the north bank and by Asia Minor on the south. The Hellespont is only 38 miles long and between three-quarters of a mile and four miles wide.

Many famous castles overlook the strait including the Old Castle of Anatolia and the Old Castle of Rumelia. The strait has long been prominent in history. The army of the Persian king Xerxes crossed it by a bridge of boats. This expedition against the Greeks probably explains the origin of the name Hellespont: "Helles" comes from "Hellenic" or "of the Greeks" and "pont" means "bridge".

During the First World War, the Hellespont was the scene of much fierce fighting.

FINGAL'S CAVE

The great cave named after the legendary Celtic hero Finn Mac-Cool, or Fingal, is at the southern end of the isle of Staffa, seven miles west of Mull, one of the larger islands of the Inner Hebrides off Scotland's west coast. Fingal's Cave is 227 feet long, 42 feet wide and 66 feet high.

The entrance is an arch supported by basaltic pillars of awe-inspiring symmetry and, from there to the cave's end, there is a pavement of broken pillars. These pillars, either hexagonal (six-sided) or pentagonal (five-sided), form colonnaded walls elsewhere on the south and west of Staffa. The

71-acre island's name means Pillar Island in Norse.

Apart from its natural splendour, the cave is famous for its "music", heard from afar when heavy seas are running. Air, raised to a pressure of several tons to the square inch by the driving force of the sea surging into the cave, rushes out through cracks and fissures in the rock when the water recedes. This creates the musical sounds which have been described by some visitors as "like trumpets blowing". The composer Mendelssohn was inspired by this music as well as by the grandeur of Staffa in writing his *Hebrides* overture.

WILL O' THE WISP

The will o' the wisp is a pale flame, usually seen flickering over marshy ground. Another name for it is jack o' lantern. The phrase is often used in ghost or fairy stories to help create an atmosphere of mystery.

No one quite knows what causes will o' the wisp. Scientists think it is produced by gases catching alight in the air. These gases are probably formed by dead plant or animal matter, rotting in the ground. This would explain why the will o' the wisp tends to appear in such localities as stagnant marshes and damp moorlands.

WHERE is the Emerald Isle? WHERE does gold come from?

EMERALD ISLE

This is a romantic name for Ireland, the second largest of the British Isles, which is farther into the Atlantic Ocean and the warm Gulf Stream current than its bigger neighbour to the east. The moist prevailing westerly winds bring between 30 and 50 inches of rainfall each year and maintain a temperature ranging between 0° and 21° Centigrade. All this gives the countryside a rare greenness— hence its popular description as the Emerald Isle.

Ireland

West coast of England

GOLD SOURCES

The main gold-producing regions of the world are in the Republic of South Africa, Ghana, Southern Rhodesia, the Congo, the Soviet Union, Canada, the United States, Australia, Columbia and the Philippines.

Many wars of ancient times were fought principally to secure gold as loot. Alexander the Great brought back vast quantities of gold from his Persian expeditions. During the Middle Ages alchemists sought the Philosopher's Stone, which would turn base metals into gold.

Exploration was stimulated by the search for the metal. The promise of it from the Indies helped Columbus to get support for his expedition. Spanish gold from Mexico and Peru greatly increased the stock held in Europe. Rich deposits were discovered in Colombia and Brazil in the 18th and 19th Centuries, and these were the world's chief sources of supply for 200 years.

In 1848 a gold strike was made in California and hundreds of thousands of men poured into the Golden West. Many died, but some survivors became very rich, for California was soon yielding £10 million worth of gold every year. In 1851 new veins were found in Australia. The third great gold rush of the century occurred in 1896, when the Klondike gold-field was discovered in the far north-west of Canada.

The world's richest known source was discovered in 1884 in South Africa, near what is now Johannesburg. This is the great gold-bearing reef of the Witwatersrand which has produced more than £4,000 million worth of gold. Its annual output is more than half the world's total supply.

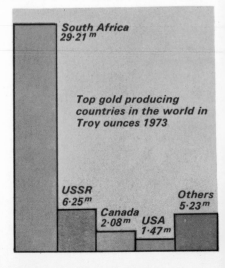

South Africa
29·21ᵐ

Top gold producing countries in the world in Troy ounces 1973

USSR
6·25ᵐ

Canada
2·08ᵐ

USA
1·47ᵐ

Others
5·23ᵐ

WHERE is Alice Springs?

ALICE SPRINGS

Alice Springs is a town situated in the heart of the continent of Australia, centred in the lower third of the Northern Territory.

The surrounding countryside, "the Centre" as Australians call it, is parched. The lakes and rivers are dry for most of the time and the cattlemen on the few homesteads depend on water pumped from bores hundreds of feet deep.

The town of Alice Springs was founded in the middle of the 19th Century after the discovery of a sheltered, watered plain among the MacDonnell Ranges, a series of hills which ripple for 250 miles across the land. By 1872 a telegraph station had been built at a water hole beneath a rocky hill. It was called Alice Springs after the wife of Charles Todd, superintendent of telegraphs in Adelaide, but it is always known as Alice to Australians.

Next came prospectors looking for gold. They left a ghost town at Arltunga not far from Alice. Once, back in 1880, they thought they had found rubies by the million, but the gems proved to be cheap garnets, not worth transporting. Cattlemen soon followed, for much of "the Centre" is marginal land that provides good feed when it rains. They knew the rains did not come often, but felt one good season could carry five bad seasons. Often it has had to carry seven or eight bad ones.

The growth of Alice Springs in recent years has astonished everybody. The railroad linked it to Adelaide in 1939 when its population was less than 100. By the Second World War 1,000 people lived there. It was used as a military base after the Japanese bombed Darwin. Stuart Highway — still called simply "the bitumen" —

was completed from Darwin to Alice, a distance of 954 miles.

Today, Alice Springs is a prosperous town of 6,000 people. It attracts crowds of tourists especially during the fine winter weather from June to September. They come for the spectacular scenery, the famous aboriginal artists, and to visit surrounding cattle stations.

Attractions include the tremendous monolith of Ayers Rock which towers 1,143 feet above the plain and is six miles around — the biggest "pebble" in the world, surrounded by a flat desert.

Since the 1950s the area has been suffering from the worst drought people can remember. It is feared that "the Centre" may turn into a huge dustbowl. So it looks as if the future of Alice Springs lies in its tourist trade and the mineral wealth which experts believe lies under the rugged landscape.

WHERE is the Dust Bowl? WHERE is the deepest part of th

THE DUST BOWL

The name Dust Bowl was given to the man-made desert in the central United States in the 1930s. There dust storms blew which were as severe as any on record. One storm in 1933 was traced for 1,300 miles to northern New York.

For the origin of the Dust Bowl we must go back to the late 1800s when homesteaders were advancing relentlessly towards the west and planting their crops in the short-grass country, land known previously as the American desert. The farmers brought with them strains of hard winter wheat that were resistant to drought, disease and insects. They ploughed into the thin grassland and sowed the seeds both of wheat and tragedy.

The states involved were western Texas, Oklahoma, Kansas, Nebraska and North and South Dakota to the Pacific coast. Wheat was the principal crop. Dry farming techniques were developed. These enabled farmers to conserve the meagre moisture in the soil by a process of dust mulching and by permitting the land to lie fallow to build up moisture for the following crop year. However, the farmers did not know how to conserve their soil and prevent the erosion of semi-arid earth which had been anchored only by the cover-crop of thin grass.

The great drought of 1932–7 led to the Dust Bowl and caused the abandonment of vast areas of land. Many people left their farms for California, where they joined other migratory workers in search of jobs as fruit and vegetable pickers.

Meanwhile the American government, with Franklin D Roosevelt as president, took action to aid the ravaged area. Starving cattle were moved to better ranges, or bought and slaughtered. Loans were extended to the distressed farmers. Mortgage foreclosures were stopped in 1933 by the extension of government credit. Soil erosion was attacked by encouraging farmers to use more effective methods of keeping their land in condition, and a great irrigation programme was begun.

OCEAN DEPTH

The deepest part of the ocean is the Marianas Trench off the Philippine Islands in the South Pacific. There the sea floor lies 36,198 feet below the waves. So the distance to the surface is more than a mile greater than the height of Mount Everest.

Jacques Piccard and Lt. Donald Walsh descended to the bottom of the Marianas Trench on January 23, 1960 in the United States Navy bathyscaphe Trieste. It took four and a half hours to make the trip to the bottom, where the water pressure was eight tons to the square inch. This is the nearest men have come to making a journey to the centre of the earth.

The average depth of water in the world's oceans is 12,000 feet. But, apart from the Marianas Trench, there are other trenches in the seabed more than six miles deep.

The floor of the ocean is, of course, as well defined with canyons and "mountain" peaks as the dry land of the earth, something we do not normally consider when we look at the ocean surface.

The imposing facade of St. Peter's in the Vatican.

SMALLEST COUNTRY

The smallest country in the world is the Vatican City. The Vatican is an independent and sovereign state within the boundaries of Rome in Italy.

Although the Vatican has always been the spiritual and administrative centre of the Roman Catholic Church, it did not become an independent state until 1929.

The city state has a daily newspaper, a railway station, and its own bank. It has an area of 0·17 square miles and a population of 1,000.

There are no frontier formalities for those entering Vatican City where millions yearly visit St Peter's and the exhibition galleries.

The chief treasures to be seen are the Michelangelo frescoes in the Sistine Chapel, paintings by Raphael, Fra Angelico and Caravaggio, the fescoes of Pinturicchio and the Codex Vaticanus of the Greek Bible.

ocean? WHERE is the smallest country in the world?
WHERE are the Everglades?

Cape
Canaveral

Lake Okeechobee

Palm Beach

Miami

The Everglades

Florida Bay

THE EVERGLADES

The Everglades are in Southern Florida in the United States. The peninsula of Florida, low lying and with a climate ranging from warm temperate to subtropical, stretches out from the American mainland towards Cuba. In the south of Florida lies the state's biggest stretch of inland water, Lake Okeechobee. Spreading south from this is the huge wet prairie called the Everglades which, after 100 miles, gives way to the mangrove forests fringing the peninsula's broad tip.

The Everglades have a slope to the south of only two inches to the mile and, along the eastern side of the great prairie, there is a river with an almost imperceptible

flow. This river, which is only a few inches deep and 50 miles wide, moves slowly towards the south. Along the west side tall cypresses, hundreds of years old, stand in the Big Cypress Swamp. The whole area is waterlogged, for beneath the peat beds there is a porous rock which soaks up water like a sponge. All this freshwater-soaked land keeps back the salt water of the Atlantic Ocean, and the excess of water flows into the sea.

Grasses grow in the shallow, slow-moving river. Tall cypress trees flourish in the swamps. The area is rich in vegetation and wild life. A primitive world, thousands of years old, continues into the present and the Americans sought

to preserve this by creating the Everglades National Park. But in spite of these efforts, civilization is destroying this primitive world. Agricultural land is being reclaimed by draining the swamps. Water is being taken from Lake Okeechobee and diverted from the river to quench the thirst of the Atlantic seaboard cities of Palm Beach and Miami. On the surface, the peaty soil dries out and becomes easily ignited tinder. Carelessly thrown cigarette ends create hundreds of fires.

As the swamps dry out and become barren, Nature's balance is destroyed and the wild life is threatened with extinction. The Everglades may well be doomed.

56

WHERE do icebergs go?   WHERE is the biggest lake in the

VANISHING ICEBERGS

Icebergs are huge masses of ice which have broken away from glaciers in the Arctic and Antarctic regions. They gradually melt away as the upper part is warmed by the sun and the lower part by the warmer waters into which they drift.

An iceberg may be as much as 250 feet high, although only one-ninth is above the surface of the sea. It can be a hazard to shipping.

The worst disaster was to a British passenger liner, the Titanic. This fine ship was thought to be unsinkable, because she had a double skin and 15 watertight compartments. In April, 1912, the liner struck an iceberg in the North Atlantic. Despite her double skin and watertight compartments she was holed and quickly sank. Of the 2,207 people on board, more than 1,500 were drowned.

BIGGEST LAKE

The world's biggest lake is Lake Superior, between America and Canada. It covers an area of nearly 32,000 square miles. But Superior is not the lake with the most water. Lake Baikal in southern Siberia has far more water, because although little over 12,000 square miles in area, it is nearly 6,000 feet deep.

Lake Superior is nearly as big as Austria. It is nearly 400 miles long and receives the drainage of about 200 rivers.

There is virtually no tide. But during autumn and winter storms, waves can reach extremely danger-ous heights. These waves are gradually eroding the shore, so the lake is slowly getting even bigger.

Owing to the lake's great in-dustrial advantages and transport facilities the water has become seriously polluted. Since 1965, however, the United States Government has made efforts to purify the great lake.

world?　**WHERE** is Surtsey?

SURTSEY

Surtsey is a volcanic island a few miles south-west of the Westman Islands which are situated off the south coast of Iceland. The island appeared as a result of a volcanic activity on November 15, 1963. The Icelanders took the infant island into their care because it appeared in their territorial waters.

They called the volcanic vent Surtur, and the island Surtsey (island of Surtur). In old Icelandic mythology Surtur was a giant who brought destructive fire from the south as a weapon in his fight with Frey, the god of fertility.

During its early life there was doubt about the island's chance of survival, and many thought it might disappear. A similar one did vanish in 1783 after erupting from the sea 65 miles south-west of Reykjavik, the Icelandic capital. Survival and long life were assured when repeated outpourings of thin flowing lava followed the first violent eruptions. The lava capped the volcano with a gently sloping regular dome which acted as a protective shield.

The arrival of Surtsey was no real surprise. For the 10,000-mile Mid-Atlantic Ridge, of which Iceland forms the largest above-sea land mass, had been active along its length for some years up to 1963, although since then things seem to have settled down, although further activity is always possible. The neighbouring Westman Islands were produced by volcanic activity 8,000 years ago.

WHERE is nought longitude? WHERE is Tristan da Cunha?

LONGITUDE

Nought degrees longitude passes through Greenwich on the River Thames in London, England. 0° longitude is known as the "prime meridian". You can see at Greenwich the prime meridian mark from which all countries have reckoned longitude since 1884.

Longitude and latitude are fixed lines crossing the globe by which the location of any place on the earth's surface can be determined and described.

Lines of longitude go from north to south. All start at the North Pole and end at the South Pole. Longitude is measured both 180° east and 180° west of the meridian, the two together making the full 360° of the earth's circumference.

World time is also measured from Greenwich. Greenwich Mean Time is zero hour and, depending on whether you are west or east of the prime meridian, you are either so many hours behind or ahead of the time of Greenwich.

The Royal Observatory at Greenwich was founded in 1675 and was one of Sir Christopher Wren's great designs. In 1960 the building was opened as an astronomical museum.

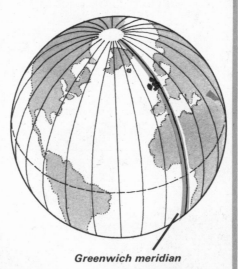

Greenwich meridian

TRISTAN DA CUNHA

Tristan da Cunha is one of five small and remote islands in the South Atlantic midway between Buenos Aires in Argentina and the Cape of Good Hope, South Africa. Tristan is the only one of the five to be inhabited.

The island is 37 square miles in extent and was named after the Portuguese admiral who discovered it in 1506. Tristan da Cunha was created in prehistoric times when a volcanic eruption raised it 18,000 feet from the seabed. Cultivation is possible only on one part of the rocky outcrop, on a small plateau squeezed between the sea on one side and 2,000 foot cliffs on the other.

In 1816 Britain landed a small force of men on the island and took possession. The garrison stayed for a year. When it departed, one of its members, Corporal William Glass, was allowed to remain on Tristan with his family.

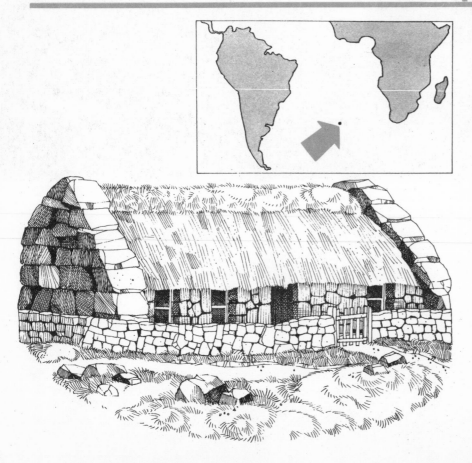

WHERE is Oberammergau?

With the arrival of shipwrecked sailors and of five women from St Helena, the population grew to 260 by 1961.

For 150 years the islanders' way of life changed little. But in 1961 the volcano erupted and forced their departure to England. This evacuation seemed to be the end of life on Tristan but, weary of contact with modern civilization and longing for their island ways, the people began to return two years later.

The Tristan da Cunha Development Company now provides the island's sole industry. By 1967 Tristan had a small harbour for the first time in its history. After that a road, a new hospital and a sewage system were built, and electricity was introduced. The island now has something approaching the best of both worlds, isolation and "away from it all" atmosphere but some modern amenities, too.

OBERAMMERGAU

Oberammergau is a small village in the Bavarian Alps near Germany's border with Austria.

In the winter of 1632 the village was struck by the Black Plague, which spread devastation through Europe. By the following summer one-eighth of Oberammergau's population of 1,000 people had died.

The village elders called all those who could walk to the church and everyone made a vow: "A solemn promise to devote one year in 10 to the preparation and presentation of the tragedy of our Lord's Passion to keep the Christian principle of the redemption of the world before men for all time."

There were no more deaths from the plague, and the villagers believed God had heard their vow.

Apart from an occasional lapse, due in the main to wars, the village people of Oberammergau have presented their Passion Play every 10 years. The first performance was held in the church in 1634. Nowadays a huge theatre, looking rather like a great aircraft hangar, is used. It seats 6,000 people and has room on the stage for crowd scenes with 500 actors. Only native-born villagers may be considered for the 600 parts in the play. Selection for the principal parts is made by ballot more than 12 months before the performance. Rehearsals begin in May for the first performance in May of the following year.

The Passion Play has given Oberammergau worldwide renown and visitors travel long distances to see the eight-hour play.

The play is divided into episodes. These episodes are introduced by the Passion chorus, which consists of fifty singers.

The whole community becomes involved in the production in a completely medieval way.

HIGHEST MOUNTAIN

The world's highest mountain is Mount Everest, on the Nepal–Tibet frontier in the eastern Himalayas. Mount Everest was named after Sir George Everest who discovered it in 1856, when he was surveyor-general of India. At that time its height was estimated by trigonometry as 29,002 feet, but more recently it has been established as 29,028 feet.

Everest is not only the highest mountain in the world, but also the most magnificent and inaccessible. It is swept by icy winds and gripped in a coldness that often drops far below zero. There are great glaciers and crevasses, ice-

falls and sheer rock faces, and the rarified atmosphere at its greatest heights has defied generations of climbers.

It was not until 1920 that the Dalai Lama of Tibet was persuaded to permit a British climbing party into his territory. Until then both Nepal and Tibet had forbidden any such intrusion.

Several unsuccessful British expeditions were made to conquer the mountain and 16 men were lost in the attempts. In 1951 Eric Shipton made an approach from the south through Nepal. Before then all the expeditions had made their approach from the north.

Shipton had no intention of attempting an assault on the summit. His object was to gather information for future expeditions.

With the help of this information a British expedition, using light-weight oxygen-breathing apparatus and other weight-saving equipment, reached the summit in 1953. It was led by Colonel H. C. J. Hunt, later Lord Hunt.

Nine camps were made during the climb, and on the morning of May 29 a New Zealander, Edmund Hillary, and Sherpa Tensing Norkey made the final assault. At 11.30 a.m., after a hard climb, they reached the summit.

argest reef in the world?
WHERE do thunderbolts come from?

LARGEST REEF

The largest reef in the world is the Great Barrier Reef off the north-east corner of Australia. From Anchor Cay (or island) above the northern tip of Queensland, the reef runs parallel to the mainland at a distance of about 60 miles, to Lady Elliot Island, 1,250 miles away to the south.

This reef, which is 80,000 square miles in area, was discovered in 1770 by Captain Cook. He called one of the many navigable passages Providential Channel after he had edged his ship through it to the coast. He named Endeavour Reef, where he ran aground, after the ship itself.

The fantastic coral forms give shelter to a collection of other living creatures, such as fish, crustaceans, worms, molluscs and starfish, of greater variety than can be found anywhere else. Ninety per cent of the reef is under water and the remainder is composed of some 200 islands dotted along its length. A few of these islands remain permanently dry and swarm with bird life. They are used also by turtles who come ashore to lay their eggs.

The Great Barrier Reef is a delicately balanced system suffering, from time to time, an upset in its regular routine. Such an upset began in the 1960s with the invasion of the large poison-spined starfish, which is still going on. Appropriately called "crown-of-thorns", this starfish has infested some parts of the reef and by feeding on the polyps has ravaged vast areas of living coral. Even so, the reef remains one of the most colourful regions of the world.

THUNDERBOLTS

Thunderbolts are actually lightning. A thundercloud forms when air carries moisture high into the sky. Raindrops form, and the movement of air currents causes them to be charged with electricity. When the charges become strong enough lightning flashes within the cloud. If the charge cannot be contained in the cloud the lightning flashes to earth with a loud clap, and a tree or other tall object on the ground may be struck and sometimes destroyed.

Occasionally the lightning fuses metal or sand, producing a hard, rough object which the ancients used to think was hurled down from the sky by an angry god. This was the so-called "thunderbolt". The word is now used to describe a sudden or overwhelming occurrence.

WHERE is the oldest republic? **WHERE** was the greatest

volcanic eruption?

OLDEST REPUBLIC

The tiny country of San Marino, a few miles from Rimini on the Adriatic coast and surrounded by Italy, set up its own government in the 10th Century. This makes San Marino the oldest surviving republic in the world.

According to legend it was founded in the 4th Century by Marinus, a stone cutter from Dalmatia (now part of Yugoslavia). He fled to a mountain retreat, Monte Titano, to escape persecution by the Roman Emperor Diocletian.

Marinus bequeathed this retreat to his followers to remain evermore as an island of liberty in a tyrannical world. The republic's capital, San Marino, is built around the three craggy tops of Monte Titano, which rises to a height of 2,425 feet almost in the centre of the country's 24 square miles.

Over the centuries the republic has been invaded several times but has always regained its independence. In 1861, the people of San Marino, considerate of others, wrote to Abraham Lincoln expressing their concern over the troubles in America. An appreciative Lincoln wrote back: "Although your dominion is small, your state is nevertheless one of the most honoured in history."

Napoleon had offered this "model of a republic" additional territory in 1797, but San Marino declined to accept it.

The inhabitants are of Italian origin but they have one big problem. Over the centuries the families of the republic became so inter-related that the citizens found it impossible to provide a completely impartial system of law enforcement. Because of this they decided to "import" their judges and police forces from Italy. In this way the San Merino families have avoided feuds and family charges of favouritism.

VOLCANIC ERUPTION

The greatest volcanic eruption, in modern times, was on an island in the Sundra Strait between Sumatra and Java. On August 27, 1883, the volcano of Krakatoa suddenly erupted with a tremendous explosion that has been estimated to be the equivalent of 26 large atomic bombs. Rocks and ash were hurled up to 12 miles in the air and over half of the island was blown away. More than 160 villages were destroyed and 36,000 people were killed by 120-foot-high waves which were caused by the explosion.

The sound of the eruption was clearly heard four hours later nearly 3,000 miles away. Dust and ashes fell, days later, on Singapore and southern Java. Clouds of volcanic dust thrown high into the atmosphere travelled round the world and caused spectacular sunsets, even as far away as western Europe.

In the eruptions, which lasted two days, the highest part of the island became a huge crater which was filled by the sea. The remaining part was covered with layers of lava and ash which stayed hot for weeks.

No life was left on the island. But a small monkey was rescued from a floating piece of wood in the Sundra Strait. She was badly burned, but had survived one of the worst volcanic disasters ever recorded in history.

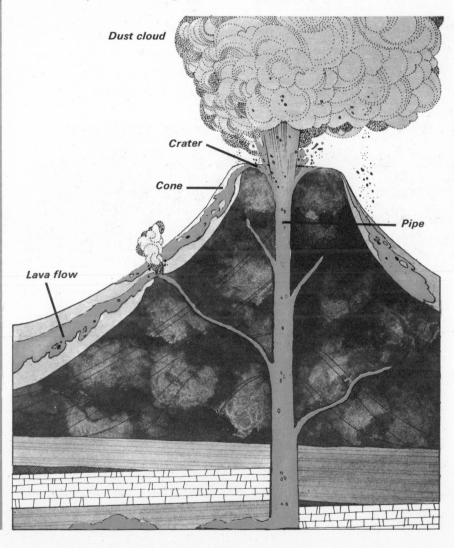

Dust cloud

Crater

Cone

Pipe

Lava flow

WHERE is the Kremlin? WHERE is Easter Island? WHERE

THE KREMLIN

The Kremlin was the palace of the Russian Tsars in Moscow until Peter the Great (1672–1725) moved the whole imperial court to the newly-founded city of St Petersburg (now Leningrad) early in the 18th Century.

In 1922 Moscow was chosen as the capital of the Union of Soviet Socialist Republics. Once again the Kremlin became the headquarters of government.

Encircled by great battlements erected in the 15th Century, the citadel covers an area of 65 acres and is almost a city itself. Around the walls are 19 towers and five gates, the finest of them being Spasskaya (Saviour's) Tower and Gate which houses the Kremlin chimes. Men used to doff their hats as they passed by this gate in Red Square.

Within the walls are churches, four cathedrals and many palaces. In 1955 the Kremlin was opened to the public and the palaces now exhibit the riches of Tsarist days.

Outside the walls is Red Square, 900 yards long by 175 yards wide, where the great military parades are held annually to commemorate the revolution of 1917. The embalmed body of Lenin (1870–1924), leader of the revolution, lies in its mausoleum in front of the Kremlin's wall.

The defensive fortresses at the centre of many medieval Russian cities were also called Kremlin, which is where the word comes from.

s Magyar spoken officially?

EASTER ISLAND

Easter Island, one of the most mysterious islands in the world, is in the South Pacific, 2,000 miles west of Caldera in Chile and 1,000 miles east of Pitcairn, its nearest inhabited neighbour. It was annexed by Chile in 1888. The island which is volcanic in origin, was discovered by the Dutch admiral Jacob Roggeveen on Easter Sunday, 1722. It is 11 miles long and 15 miles wide.

Easter Island is noted for its mysterious statues of remote and unknown origin. These statues, consisting of giant heads facing inland, fringe the island's coastline. They stand on huge ramparts or platforms which slope landwards, in some cases to a width of 250 feet. At the end of this sloping rampart there is a paved area.

There are some 260 of these platforms on the island and each one was designed to support between one and 15 of the strange giant heads, carved from compressed volcanic earth. The heads have upturned faces tilted towards the sky, and long ears. They vary in height from 12 to 20 feet. At one time they were topped by huge hats or crowns between six and eight feet in diameter. These hats are made from a red volcanic material different from the material used for the heads themselves.

The island is full of ancient curiosities including long, narrow boat-shaped houses flanked by stone chicken huts. The inhabitants are descendants of Polynesian people who migrated across the Pacific.

There is a legend of a war between the "long-eared" people and their "short-eared" attackers. The long-eared defenders of the island were said to have been burned in a vast earth oven, but the latest scientific evidence suggests that the "earth oven" was in fact a vast defensive ditch. Ashes in this ditch date from the 17th Century, only a short time before the island's discovery.

But the real truth about Easter Island and its mysterious statues will probably never be known until someone finds out how to read the curious sign language inscribed round the platforms. These signs, which are geometrical in form, are really symbols such as birds, plants and fishes. They may be like the "memory aids" of the ancient Aztecs, but experts believe they are an elementary form of writing.

MAGYAR LANGUAGE

The Magyar language is the official language of Hungary (or, in the Magyar language, the country of Magyarorszaq). In 1967 the population was 10,197,000 with another two million Magyar-speaking people living outside Hungary—mainly in Czechoslovakia, Rumania and Yugoslavia. Nearly half a million Magyars live in the United States of America.

Magyar belongs to the Arabic language family. Apart from Finland, where the language is closely related to Hungarian, the only part of the world where you are likely to hear anything similar is in western Siberia.

Because several suffixes, or smaller words, are often added, the Magyars can produce words of considerable length. For instance, "the very biggest" would be "legeslegnagyobb" in Magyar.

The first written example of Magyar dates from about 1200, when a short funeral oration was recorded.

WHERE are the Pillars of Hercules? WHERE does sulphu

PILLARS OF HERCULES

The Pillars of Hercules are on either side of the Strait of Gibraltar. The legendary Greek hero Hercules was said to have erected the Pillars on a journey to capture the Oxen of Geryon, a monster with three heads who lived on an Atlantic island. Passing out of the Mediterranean he threw up the rocks on either side of the Strait of Gibraltar. They were the Rock of Gibraltar and the headland on the Moroccan side.

Hercules' journey was one of the 12 labours that the son of Zeus had been set by Eurystheus, King of Tiryns, whose servant he had become. One of the most famous of these labours was the cleansing of the Augean stables. So innumerable were the herds of cattle that used these stables that, as they returned from pasture, they seemed to reach endlessly across the plain. Their stables were heaped high with manure and had not been cleaned for years. Hercules diverted the Rivers Alpheus and Pereus through them, and completed the task in one day.

For his last labour he braved the Underworld to capture Cerberus, its three-headed watchdog.

The great promontory of Gibraltar, known to the ancient Greeks as one of the Pillars of Hercules.

HIGHEST WATERFALL

The world's highest waterfall is in Venezuela, South America. It is known as the Angel Falls and lies on the River Carrao. This magnificent waterfall tumbles 3,212 feet down to the river.

The Venezuelans did not even know about Angel Falls or the surrounding country until the 1930s, because steep rocks made overland travel to the region impossible. It was not until aircraft started penetrating the region that the falls were discovered.

The falls get their name from the United States adventurer and explorer James Angel who crashed near them in an aeroplane in 1935.

ORIGIN OF SULPHUR

Sulphur is a volcanic product. It has many industrial uses. The volcanoes of Sicily and Japan were once the world's chief suppliers.

Today important sources are in Texas and Louisiana in the United States. In the coastal regions there are underground sulphur domes. Two pipes, one inside the other, are forced down to the domes.

Superheated steam is pumped down one of the pipes, melting the sulphur which is then forced up the other pipe. This method provides 92 per cent of the United States output.

The other source is from sulphides of various metals which are called "pyrites". It is the main source of sulphur in Sicily and Japan today.

me from? **WHERE** is the world's highest waterfall? **WHERE** do countries get their names from?

NAMING THE NATIONS

Countries do not all have universally accepted names. Holland is officially The Netherlands. Finland is called Suomi by its own people. The names of countries often spring from the discoverer and sometimes from a native tribe or even a conquering people. America is named after Amerigo Vespucci, the explorer, France after the Frankish invaders, and England after the Angles.

The Greeks and Romans called England "Albion"—which is probably derived from *albus* meaning white and is a reference to her white cliffs—the first things the Romans would have seen on their arrival. Spain in Spanish is Espana and in Latin, Hispania. An amusing story of the origin of Quebec in Canada is that it was so called because the French sailors who first saw the rocky promontory cried: "Quel bec!" or "What a beak!"

The white cliffs of Dover, England. "Albus" is the Latin word for white, hence the name of "Albion" for England.

Reindeer crossing a frozen lake in Finland known to the Fins as Suomi (derived from suomaa, the damp and frozen land).

Iceland's name derivation is self-explanatory—yet the island is also famous for its natural hot geysers!

WHERE is the world's biggest desert?   WHERE is the Gran

Trees and vegetation appear gradually around the edge of the desert.

BIGGEST DESERT

The world's largest desert is the great desert of North Africa: the Sahara. "Sahara" in Arabic means wilderness, and this wilderness stretches right across Africa from the Atlantic Ocean to the Red Sea. From east to west it covers more than 3,000 miles. East of the Red Sea, desert conditions continue through Saudi Arabia into Persia.

To calculate the Sahara's breadth is not so easy. The desert does not simply "stop", and vege-

tation begin from that point on. Indeed desert conditions disappear so gradually that nowhere to the south does it have precise boundaries. Nevertheless, the Sahara is seldom less than 1,000 miles wide, and consequently must have an area exceeding three million square miles. These enormous dimensions make the Sahara almost as big as the United States, including Alaska.

The Sahara is one of the hottest

regions of the world and, on average, receives only 17 days of rain a year. When it does rain, delicate herbs and flowers grow rapidly and then disappear almost as quickly as they came.

Many people think of a desert as a flat expanse of sand. But in the Sahara there are many mountains, some rising to 10,000 feet. For part of the year some of these strangely shaped peaks will even be covered in snow.

anyon? **WHERE** is the wettest place on earth?

GRAND CANYON

The Grand Canyon is in the northern part of Arizona in the United States. It is a tremendous gorge cut into the high plateau by the Colorado River. In some places it is 18 miles wide. At its deepest parts it goes down a mile below its rim.

The canyon is breathtaking to look at, partly because it is so huge, but also because of the colours of the rocks. The main colour is dull red, but other rocks are violet, pale pink, green and dark brown.

The canyon is an interesting place for geologists to study rocks, because it contains examples from many different periods of time. The rocks are marked by weather, earth movement, and water. Many animal fossils have been found there, including the remains of dinosaurs and elephants.

The most beautiful part of the canyon is the National Park, which was created in 1919.

WETTEST PLACE

The wettest place in the world is Kauai, one of the Hawaiian Islands.

Mont Wai, which is 5,000 feet high, is the wettest point of the island. Records over a period of 30 years showed that an average of only 14 days a year had no rain. During that time the average yearly rainfall was over 480 inches.

Kauai, west of Hawaii's capital Honolulu, is on the same latitude as the southern tip of the Sahara Desert.

WHERE is the "Moho"—or Mohorovicic discontinuity?

THE MOHO

The Mohorovicic discontinuity is to be found between the earth's crust and the earth's mantle. Mohorovicic was a famous Croatian scientist, a seismologist.

He specialized in the composition of the earth, and particularly in earthquakes and in faults in the structure of the earth, which are the cause of earthquakes.

Mohorovicic made a most important discovery. Scientists knew that the earth is made up of a series of layers, rather like an onion. There are many of these layers, all of different materials and all in a different state of development. The main layers are called the crust, the mantle, the liquid core and the solid core.

The great pressures inside the earth force the weaker areas of the rocky layers out of alignment and this pushing, twisting movement is experienced as an earthquake on the surface. These great forces set up a series of waves throughout the various layers of the earth known as seismic waves.

Mohorovicic discovered a curious fact about the behaviour of these earth waves or tremors. He noticed that the shock waves travel comparatively slowly through the actual crust of the earth. But when they reach the lowest level of the crust—the layer called basaltic rock which rests on the next layer called the mantle—the waves increase dramatically in speed. Sometimes they also change direction.

This curious fact was proved by Mohorovicic's experiments. The importance of his discovery was that it proved the earth's crust is different from the mantle beneath.

So the "Mohorovicic discontinuity" is the scientific term used to describe this strange behaviour of the earth's shock waves.

Usually this level of the earth's composition is called the Moho since even scientists found Mohorovicic's name difficult to pronounce! By plotting these earth waves on sensitive shock recording machines known as seismographs we have found that most of the outer crust of the earth is between 20 and 25 miles thick in continental areas, but only three miles thick under some oceans.

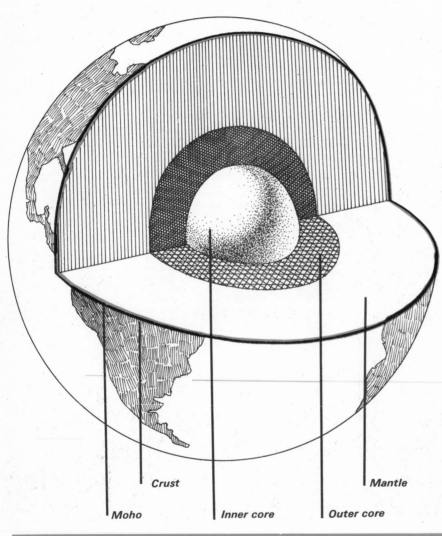

Crust

Mantle

Moho

Inner core

Outer core

THE MISTRAL

This is the name given to a wind which blows in the Rhône Valley in France. The wind is caused by an exchange of air between the cold hinterland of France's Central Plateau and the warm Gulf of the Lion in the Mediterranean Sea.

High mountain ranges near flat country produce unpleasant winds, especially where the mountains descend to a warm sea. Atmospheric pressure is high above the cold mountains, but low above the sea. Air, therefore, flows towards the sea and is not warmed because it has not crossed enough land.

The north-westerly mistral, funnelling down the constriction of the Rhône Valley, blows at a speed of 30 to 60 m.p.h. on at least 50 days each year. It bursts out on to the Mediterranean coast, filling holidaymakers' caravans with sand and capsizing yachts caught unaware at sea.

WHERE is the mistral? WHERE is the Gulf Stream?

GULF STREAM

The Gulf Stream is in the Atlantic. It is a warm ocean current which flows steadily from the Gulf of Mexico north-eastwards. One branch reaches the Canary Islands, turns southwards and moves back across the South Atlantic. The other branch flows past the western coasts of northern Europe.

This current, which is like a river in the sea, is 50 miles wide at its narrowest and nearly 2,000 feet deep. It sweeps along with it many forms of warm water life from the tropics, but these die before they reach the European coasts where the warm water mixes with cold water moving down from the Arctic.

The Gulf Stream has a great effect on the weather of Britain and Norway. The prevailing south-westerly winds are warmed by it and collect moisture which turns into rain. In winter the warm water keeps open the cold northern ports, such as Hammerfest, in Norway, and Murmansk, in the Soviet Union, while harbours in the Baltic, many miles farther south, are blocked with ice. In summer it causes bright flowers to bloom on the west coast of Spitzbergen 500 miles north of Norway. In contrast, the east coast, cooled by Arctic water, is bleak and colourless.

In 1912 the United States Congress was asked for money to build a jetty which, it was thought, would divert the Gulf Stream and make it flow up the east coast of the United States. Although this scheme was unlikely to be successful, it was just as well for Britain and Norway that it was never tried. Without the Gulf Stream, Britain's winters would be very much longer and colder, and Norway's harbours, which are vital to the country, would be frozen over for many months.

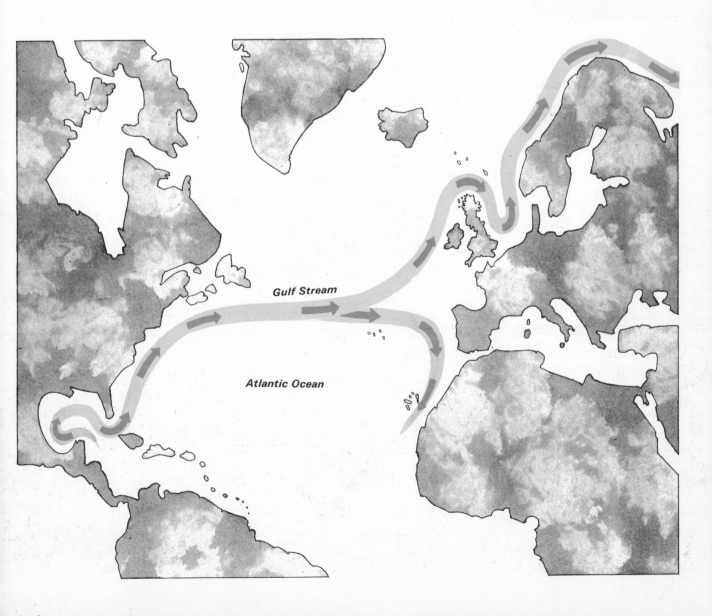

Gulf Stream

Atlantic Ocean

WHERE is the world's largest island—apart from Australia?

WHERE is the driest place on earth?
WHERE is the hottest place on earth?

LARGEST ISLAND

The largest island in the world is Greenland—if we exclude mainland Australia, which ranks as a continent.

Most of Greenland, which has an area of 840,000 square miles, lies within the Arctic circle. More than 708,000 square miles are covered with ice. Greenland is about 1,650 miles long and nearly 800 miles wide. In the extreme north it is separated only by a 25-mile wide strait from the Canadian Arctic archipelago.

The island is divided into two natural regions. One is the coastal region, where the mountains rise out of the ice. The other is the ice sheet, which covers more than four-fifths of the country, burying all valleys and mountains far below its surface. The highest mountain in Greenland is Mount Gunnbjorn which rises up to 12,139 feet. As the whole country lies north of the tree line there are no forests, but in the south-west groups of trees do grow up to 10 feet in height.

The polar climate is uncertain and changes suddenly from bright sunshine to dense fog or heavy falls of snow. Temperatures can vary from 10° Centigrade (50° Fahrenheit) in July on the coast to about —47° Centigrade (—52·6° Fahrenheit) in the interior. The lowest recorded temperature in winter was —65° Centigrade (—85° Fahrenheit).

Greenland forms a part of the Danish kingdom. In 1960 its population was 33,140. The islanders speak both Danish and Eskimo.

DRIEST PLACE

The driest place on earth is to be found in Chile in the Atacama Desert at Calama. Weather reports for Chile date only from the Spanish conquest about 400 years ago. In those last 400 years not one drop of rain has fallen.

This part of the Deisorto de Atacama has suffered the longest drought in recorded history. Strangely, Chile also has one of the wettest places on earth. Not too far from the Atacama Desert is Bahia Felix. In 1916 it rained there on every day of the year.

HOTTEST PLACE

For sheer consistency the hottest place in the world is Lugh Ganane in Somalia, east Africa, where the temperature never falls below about 31° Centigrade (88° Fahrenheit.

However, the hottest temperature ever recorded was in 1933 at San Luis Potosi in Mexico where about 58° Centigrade (136° Fahrenheit) in the shade was recorded.

In California in 1917 temperatures about 49° Centigrade (120° Fahrenheit) were recorded on 43 consecutive days—in Death Valley, not surprisingly.

Western Australia also has more than its fair share of sunshine. At Marble Bar, for instance, the temperature remained around 100°F for 160 days and in 1946 at Wyndham, again in Western Australia, the temperature reached 90°F or more, for almost the whole year (333 days to be exact).

SARGASSO SEA

The Sargasso Sea is in the Atlantic Ocean south of the Bermudas and several hundred miles east of the American mainland. It is famous for its seaweed and as a spawning ground for eels.

When these eels are eight or more years old and spawning time is due, they leave the pond or stream where they have been living and make their way, over land if necessary, to the sea.

When they reach the area known as the Sargasso, the females lay their millions of eggs at a depth of 1,500 feet and the males fertilize them. The baby eels hatch out after a few days and float to the surface. Vast masses of seaweed lie on the surface of the Sargasso.

Carried along by winds and ocean currents from the Gulf of Mexico and Caribbean Sea, this floating seaweed is concentrated into an area many thousands of square miles in extent. There it gives refuge to myriads of sea creatures, such as fish, sea-worms, molluscs, crabs and jellyfish. Sea birds find it useful as a resting place.

This floating "island" may have given rise to the famous legend in ancient times of the lost land of Atlantis. Christopher Columbus recorded taking two weeks to sail through it in 1492.

But what happens to the baby eels? Drifting at first, they eventually make their way to the ponds and streams of their parents. The American eels go to America and the European eels to Europe. The old eels do not return but die after spawning.

The Sargasso Sea is the subject of many legends. Ships are said to have vanished in it, but there is no truth in the legend that associates it with the lost land of Atlantis.

hanging gardens in history?
WHERE is the world's saltiest sea?

HANGING GARDENS

They were created by Nebuchadnezzar (605–562 B.C.) in Babylon and were regarded as one of the Seven Wonders of the Ancient World.

Babylon, situated about 50 miles to the south of Baghdad in what is now Iraq, had long been the capital in the time of the Chaldeans. Nebuchadnezzar, who ruled for 40 years and was the greatest of the Chaldean Emperors, enlarged the city and gave it enormous protective walls.

The hanging gardens, rising in terraces to a height of some 350 feet, were built, so the legend goes, for Nebuchadnezzar's wife, Amyhia, either to please her and thereby gain the support of her father's armies against her husband's foes, or simply because she did not like the flatness of the land after the hills of her homeland.

Each terrace had sufficient earth for trees such as oak, willow, pomegranate and palm to grow, as well as shrubs and flowers. Stairways led from terrace to terrace. Water cisterns were placed at the top to irrigate the lower terraces. Today, only a few ruins remain.

Believe it or not, she really is floating!

SALTIEST SEA

The Dead Sea is in south-west Asia and is really a big lake. Its northern half belongs to Jordan and its southern half is divided between Jordan and Israel.

It covers an area of 394 square miles and contains about 11,600,000,000 tons of salt. The River Jordan, which contains only 35 parts of salt to 100,000 parts of water, flows into the Dead Sea and each year adds 850,000 tons of salt to the total.

The lake's surface level lies 1,302 feet below the Mediterranean and is the lowest sheet of water on earth. In summer the absence of rain and the high rate of evaporation cause the water level to drop between 10 and 15 feet below that in winter. There is no outlet from the Dead Sea, but water balance is maintained by evaporation. Blue-white clouds, which form a mist over the surface of the water, carry off the evaporated moisture.

The Dead Sea is mentioned many times in the Bible. It gave its name to the Dead Sea Scrolls, groups of leather manuscripts and papyri first discovered in 1947 in caves on the lake shore. These scrolls date from the time immediately before and contemporary with the rise of Christianity. (No modern cities are to be found on its shore and no traces remain of the five cities said to have been near it in Abraham's time—Sodom, Gomorrah, Admah, Zeboiim and Zoar.)

Despite the lack of hotels, tourists come to the area because of the warm climate, the sense of history and the magnificent and awe-inspiring scenery. The climax of a trip is a swim in the lake, for the water is so full of salt that it is extremely difficult to sink in it.

The minerals and salts of the Dead Sea are being exploited for industry. But the lake itself is truly dead; no fish are able to live in it.

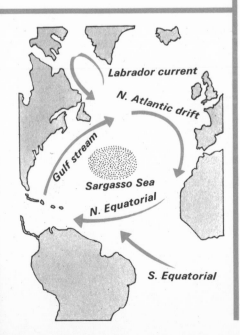

Labrador current

N. Atlantic drift

Gulf stream

Sargasso Sea

N. Equatorial

S. Equatorial

WHERE is the Golden Gate?   WHERE is the legendary land

GOLDEN GATE

The Golden Gate is the name given to the break in the long chain of mountains running down the Pacific Ocean coastline of California. This gate, or gap, forms the sea entrance to San Francisco Bay.

The gap was mapped in 1846 by John C. Frémont, an American Army officer and explorer, who named it CHRYSOPYLAE—which is Greek for Golden Gate.

The bay itself had been discovered by accident in 1769, when a Spanish explorer, Gaspar de Portola, intending to establish a mission-cum-garrison at Monterey Bay, overshot his objective by several miles.

A small settlement was gradually established until, in 1848, San Francisco became the base for the gold strike in the famous Sacramento Valley. Within a year the population increased from 2,000 to 25,000. In the latter half of the 19th Century wharves and warehouses sprang up on the bay. Houses and offices, restaurants and bars spread rapidly over the steep slopes of its hills.

Rudyard Kipling, the English author, visited San Francisco in the 1880s and found it to be "a mad city inhabited for the most part by perfectly insane people whose women are of a remarkable beauty".

The great earthquake and fire of 1906 destroyed almost a third of the city. Apart from killing 450 people, it left over 100,000 homeless and did millions of dollars worth of damage.

Even so San Francisco continued to be an increasingly important maritime centre. Now about 12,000 ships use it annually. Whether liner, small cargo boat or yacht, every vessel must sail through the Golden Gate to reach the open sea.

Landlocked San Francisco Bay extends over an area of 422 square miles, but the Gate is only two miles across at its widest point. It has a tidal flow half as big again as the water flow of the River Amazon.

In 1937 work was completed on the Golden Gate Bridge to speed traffic along the coast from San Francisco. It is one of the world's man-made marvels with a central span 4,200 feet long.

of the Long White Cloud?

LONG WHITE CLOUD

The Land of the Long White Cloud is a translation of the Polynesian name for New Zealand. In the 12th Century, bands of Polynesian adventurers voyaged thousands of miles from their Pacific islands and made landfall in the country they named Ao-tea-roa.

The descendants of those adventurers are the friendly and highly intelligent people we know as the Maoris, the original settlers of New Zealand. The land and its people were discovered and named by the Dutch navigator Abel Janszoon Tasman in 1642, although he never landed.

It was not until 1769 that a European set foot in the country. Captain James Cook, the English explorer, landed in New Zealand and then sailed on to Australia. In the next eight years he came back three times.

The first settlers were sealers, whalers and traders. In 1814 a British missionary, the Rev. Samuel Marsden, began work among the Maoris. Within six years he had been joined by a number of British emigrants, and New Zealand was made a British colony. It became a dominion in 1907.

New Zealand consists of two main islands. From the top of North Island to the bottom of South Island the country is scarcely 1,000 miles long. Nowhere is it wider than 280 miles, and usually it is much narrower. But within this compass it is a land of strange and beautiful contrasts.

New Zealand's 3,000,000 inhabitants live a life where poverty is unknown and serious crime is rare. The climate is temperate and the scenery spectacular.

It is a curious fact New Zealand has no native land animals. The ancestors of the pigs, goats, rabbits, opossums, weasels and ferrets were imported. Some of the animals—rabbits for example—have since become pests. In compensation New Zealand has a huge variety of fish and birds.

In spite of its small population, the country has produced many outstanding writers, artists, musicians and scientists and has given support and encouragement to the revival and development of Maori arts and crafts.

WHERE is Arthur's Seat? WHERE is the highest tide in the

ARTHUR'S SEAT

Arthur's Seat (822 feet) is the name given to the highest of the seven hills on or around which Edinburgh, the capital of Scotland, is built. It stands in Holyrood Park, the Royal demesne which covers 648 acres. A broad road, the Queen's Drive, about three and a half miles long, encircles it.

The view from the top of Arthur's Seat is magnificent. To the south lie the Pentland and Moorfoot Hills; the Lammermuirs, North Berwick Law and the Bass Rock in the North Sea to the east; the Firth of Forth and Fife to the north; the Forth Bridges and Ben Lomond to the west; and just below, Edinburgh Castle.

Arthur's Seat is an extinct volcano. The cultivation terraces of the Iron-Age people who once inhabited the area can still be seen on its eastern slopes.

world? **WHERE** was the first canal built?

HIGHEST TIDE

The highest tide in the world is recorded in the Bay of Fundy which is between New Brunswick and Nova Scotia in eastern Canada. There the Petitcodiac River narrows, and forces the inrushing tide to the greatest height found anywhere on earth. The difference between high water and low water in the Bay of Fundy is no less than 50 feet.

Fishermen make use of these extreme tides as you see in the illustration. They set their nets at high tide and collect their catch of fish when the tide goes down.

Tides throughout the world are caused by the varying power of the pull of the sun and the moon on the oceans. They draw the water up in a great wave, and the rotation or spin of the earth every 24 hours sends this wave round the world washing the coasts of the continents and islands. The varying shapes of the coastlines and inlets also affect the tides, and, therefore, ports and navigation.

At certain times of the month, the sun and moon are said to be in conjunction—that is, they are pulling in the same direction, which causes tides to be higher. These are called spring tides. At other times in the month, the sun and moon are in opposition, which means they are pulling against one another. Then the tides are lower and are called neap tides.

FIRST CANAL

Archaeologists believe the oldest canals in the world are those whose remains were discovered near Mandali in Iraq in 1968. They believe these canals are nearly 7,000 years old (about 5,000 B.C.).

In 500 B.C. Darius the Great, the Persian emperor, ordered a canal to be built joining the River Nile to the Red Sea. This remarkable construction was the forerunner of the modern Suez Canal.

PRECIOUS STONES

Precious stones, or gems, are minerals used for adornment, and they are found in rocks. Rocks are divided into three groups. The igneous (fire-formed) rocks may be fine-grained or coarse-grained; a very coarse-grained type, called pegmatite, is an important source of gem minerals such as diamonds. Gems are also found in the cavities of the igneous rocks granite and obsidian.

Sedimentary rocks are layered rocks and, except for turquoise and opal, are the source of very few gems. However, when the original rock contained heavy minerals—and gem minerals are heavy—pebbles of them tended to be deposited as pebbles in a river bed and such deposits form the gem gravels of Upper Burma, the "byon", and those of Ceylon, the "illam".

Metamorphic rocks – rocks which have been altered by pres-sure—are a fruitful source of gem minerals, for instance the rubies found in Burma.

There are also precious materials of animal origin—pearls from oysters, ivory from elephants and coral from the tiny sea creatures which give their name to it. There are also amber and jet, whose origin is vegetable. Amber is the fossilized resin of a coniferous tree which grew in the Eocene period. Jet is a variety of fossil wood.

Gems are found throughout the world and are prized for their rarity and beauty. Their charm may depend on transparency and depth of colour as in the ruby and emerald, on colour only as in the turquoise, on purity and "fire" as in the diamond, and on "play of colour" as in the opal.

These beautiful emeralds came from uncut stones like the one shown.

MIDNIGHT SUN

The land of the Midnight Sun is the poetical name for Norway.

In that country from the end of April to the middle of August there is no real night darkness, but a long twilight. In the most northern part, the sun never sets comland of the midnight sun? **WHERE** are the Victoria Falls?

VICTORIA FALLS

These famous falls, among the most spectacular in the world, are on the boundary between Rhodesia and Zambia in southern Africa. The falls form the most remarkable feature of the Zambezi River. They are midway up the Zambezi near the town of Livingstone, which is named after David Livingstone, the Scottish missionary and explorer, who discovered the falls in 1855.

For some distance before the Victoria Falls the Zambezi flows over a level sheet of basalt—a hard, blue volcanic rock—in a valley between sandstone hills. Curiously, the Zambezi does not increase its speed of flow as it nears the mighty falls. The water pours over an almost vertical precipice, nearly a mile wide, at a rate of between four million and 75 million gallons a minute, depending on the season. The minimum flow is between November and December and the maximum between April and May.

The Victoria Falls are wider than Niagara Falls and more than twice their height. At the highest point the water plunges 355 feet.

The only outlet for this vast force of water is a narrow channel cut in the opposing barrier wall near its western end. The river is forced through this narrow, 100-foot gorge for nearly 400 feet. This part of the Falls is aptly known as the Boiling Pot.

From the Boiling Pot the water emerges into an enormous zig-zag which forms the beginning of the Batoka Gorge, about 60 miles long.

At one time it was thought that these fantastic falls were the result of a volcanic fault in the earth. Now it is believed they are caused by the check on the natural erosion of the river bed provided by the hard basaltic rock sheets.

pletely for about two months in the summer.

In winter, however, the most northern inhabitants are not so lucky. They have no sun for two months and have to eat their lunch in twilight.

WHERE is the world's longest bridge?
WHERE are the Roaring Forties?

LONGEST BRIDGE

To measure the longest bridge in the world is not as easy as it may seem. After all, there are many different kinds of bridge. Another problem is: how do you start to measure a bridge? From its supports or simply the distance it covers over ground or over water?

There are many alternatives.

The bridge with the longest span is the Verrazano-Narrows Bridge, which stretches across the entrance to New York City from Staten Island to Brooklyn. Work on the project began on August 13, 1959. The bridge was opened to traffic on November 21, 1964. It measures 6,690 feet between supports and carries two decks, each of six lanes of traffic.

The centre span over water, is 4,260 feet, the world record. The bridge carries well over 20 million vehicles a year.

WHERE would you find whirlpools?

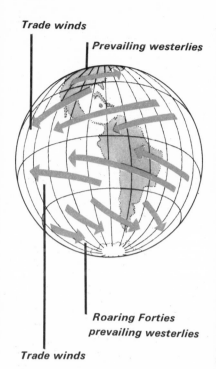

Trade winds

Prevailing westerlies

Roaring Forties prevailing westerlies

Trade winds

ROARING FORTIES

The Roaring Forties are westerly winds found between latitudes 40° and 60° South. They are prevailing winds resulting from the large, planetary circulation of the atmosphere.

The prevailing westerlies occur in both hemispheres in the middle latitudes (30°–60°), but in the Northern Hemisphere the great continental land masses of North America and Asia create a disturbance to the regular wind pattern and it is only in the Southern Hemisphere, with its small land masses, that these westerlies sweep unimpeded across the Southern oceans.

Intense, blustering, cold and often stormy, these winds were given their name by sailors who, in the days of sail, made the outward voyage to Australia by way of the Cape of Good Hope at Africa's southern tip and the return passage via Cape Horn, the southernmost tip of South America. In this way, sailing vessels would have the advantage of a following wind for both passages.

WHIRLPOOLS

Whirlpools occur quite frequently in the narrow sea passages between island groups and mainland shores. They are common in the fiords of Norway, the long, narrow inlets of sea between high cliffs.

What happens is that a rotary flow of sea currents is created by a head-on meeting of a rising tidal current with the returning ebb current of the preceding tide.

Usually whirlpools are more likely to occur over a deep or depressed area of the sea bed.

In some cases, particularly between the Sea of Japan and the Philippine Sea, the whirlpool becomes so great that the rotary flow changes to a spiralling downward flow into a deep centre. This is capable of sucking under water objects as large as ships.

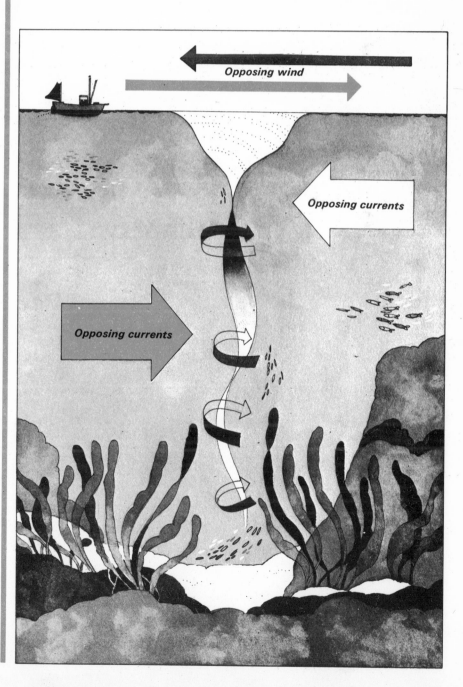

Opposing wind

Opposing currents

Opposing currents

FROST

Frost comes from the atmosphere when the temperature falls below freezing, and invisible water vapour in the air turns into white ice crystals, without first becoming a liquid. It usually occurs when the skies are clear, when there is no wind and when a mass of cold air descends on the land.

This often happens during the night in the spring and autumn of areas with temperate climates. In the morning the fields and roofs are white with what would be dew if the temperature had been above freezing point. It is the most common type of frost and is often called hoar frost.

Sometimes only the leaves of plants are fringed with white rime. This is formed when very small droplets of the moisture from fog have frozen on coming into contact with a cold object.

There is also black frost. This occurs when water vapour turns first into liquid and then freezes into a thin layer of ice instead of white crystals. As it is invisible, it is particularly dangerous when it forms on roads.

The beautiful patterns, looking like trees, ferns or feathers, which are sometimes seen on windows, are made when the water vapour in a cold room condenses.

STALACTITES

Stalactites are the stony deposits hanging like icicles from the roofs of caves. Stalagmites are similar deposits rising in columns and cones from the caves' floors.

Caves occur chiefly in limestone and chalk formations, because water dissolves these rocks. The River Lesse, for example, in its passage through the caves of Han, in Belgium, has been estimated to dissolve some five tons of limestone in a day. It is redeposited as carbonate which builds up the stalactites and stalagmites.

The seepage of water down the cave walls and through the roof produces constant dripping and evaporation. Stone icicles form on the cave roof, slowly growing with the addition of successive layers of calcium carbonate. The word "stalactite" comes from the Greek and means "drop by drop". There is, too, a general term "dripstone" which is used to cover all formations.

Stalactites are at first hollow, for the depositing of the carbonate is fastest at the outer ring of the water drop. As the evaporating water deposits its mineral matter, the cavity slowly fills up and the stalactite becomes solid. When water trickles out of a narrow cleft in the roof, instead of a small hole, a hanging curtain of stone will form in place of a conical stalactite.

If the water flows so quickly that it splashes on the floor of the cave, it deposits its calcium carbonate there and small cones and domes of stone called stalagmites begin to rise. These may grow up to join the stalactites above and form single columns. Some cave floors are covered with stalagmites. They may grow so high that they block the cave entrance.

The stalactites pictured on the right are typical specimens and show how beautiful these formations can be.

across a stalactite ?

WHERE was Morse Code first used?　**WHERE** does the lead

WHERE was the first aeroplane flown?

Science and Technology

MORSE CODE

The first message in Morse code was tapped out in the United States over a telegraph line from Baltimore to Washington by Samuel Morse in 1844.

Morse is often credited with the invention of the telegraph on his return to the United States from a trip to Europe in 1832. During this trip he became acquainted with the works of Michael Faraday on electro-magnetism, which forms the basis of the telegraph. This gave Morse the necessary impetus to go ahead with his work.

In 1837 Morse exhibited his first truly successful telegraph instrument. By 1838 he had developed the Morse code, an alphabet which consists of dots and dashes representing letters and numbers. In the same year he attempted unsuccessfully to persuade Congress to build a telegraph line.

It was not until 1843 that Congress voted to pay Morse to build the first telegraph line in the United States from Baltimore to Washington. In the following year Morse sent his famous message— "What hath God wrought!"—on this line.

Later, Morse was caught in a mass of legal claims among his telegraph partners and rival in-

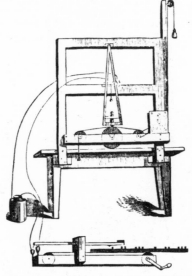

The Morse Code and original instrument.

ventors. He was probably the most successful propagator of the telegraph, although there were many pioneers in the same field long before him.

EXHAUST FUMES

The lead in exhaust fumes comes from the petrol used to drive internal-combustion engines. Crude oil straight from the wells is thick, black and sticky. It has to go through a complicated refining process before it can be used as fuel for the engines of cars, lorries, buses and aircraft.

During refining, various substances are added to improve the petrol and for other reasons. For instance, small quantities of dye are put in to standardize the colour. Other substances prevent the formation of gum which would clog up parts of the engine.

Lead, in a liquid form called tetra-ethyl lead, is added to petrol to reduce "engine knock". This means that it prevents the petrol from igniting in the engine at the wong moment. When an internal-combustion engine is running, the petrol is lit by sparks from the sparking plugs. The petrol burns in what is really a series of small explosions and produces gases which come out through the exhaust pipe as dirty, smelly fumes. And the lead comes with them.

Ill-health can be caused if quite small quantities of lead in the air are inhaled over a long time. For this reason, the governments of such countries as the United States, Britain, Sweden and Japan are passing laws to reduce the amount of lead in petrol.

They are also encouraging car manufacturers to design internal-combustion engines which will work efficiently on lead-free petrol and have cleaner exhaust fumes. These engines will be more expensive at first, but they will help to make the air cleaner and pleasanter where there is a lot of traffic.

Work is in progress to invent a satisfactory car engine that runs on alternatives to petrol, such as a battery.

exhaust fumes come from?
WHERE does candlewax go when a candle burns?

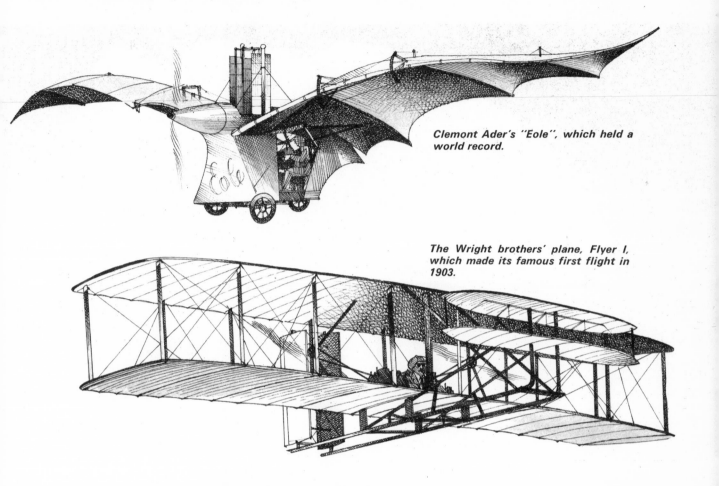

Clemont Ader's "Eole", which held a world record.

The Wright brothers' plane, Flyer I, which made its famous first flight in 1903.

FIRST AEROPLANE

The first aeroplane ever to fly was built by a French naval officer, Félix du Temple de la Croix. In 1874 his monoplane, powered with a hot-air engine, took off from the top of a hill near Brest in France. It did not get far, just a short hop, but it was a beginning. A few years later, in 1890, Clément Ader of France flew his own plane, Eole, entirely under its own power for about 50 metres. It was a world record.

The first truly successful aeroplane flight was in 1903. In December of that year Orville Wright flew his chain-driven plane Flyer I at a speed of 8 m.p.h. and at an altitude of 12 feet for 12 seconds in North Carolina, United States. It was several years before the Wrights' achievement was fully appreciated in America.

VANISHING CANDLE

Nowhere—it simply changes into other substances. That is what burning does to everything.

The moment you put a match to the wick, you start a change in the candle by turning the solid wax into a liquid. The liquid wax rises to the wick by an irresistible process called capillarity, the simplest example of which is the way blotting paper soaks up ink or water. Then the liquid wax changes into a gas which burns—a chemical reaction which releases energy in the form of light and heat.

The presence of the gas can be demonstrated by blowing out the candle and immediately holding a lighted match an inch or so above the wick. The inflammable vapour instantly catches fire, and the candle lights up again without the match having actually touched the wick.

Other changes are taking place while the candle burns. The wax is a complex chemical compound of carbon and hydrogen. The process of burning is simply the combination of the wax with the oxygen in the air. If you put a jar over the candle, it will quickly use up the oxygen and go out.

During the time the candle burns, the carbon joins with the oxygen in the air and makes carbon monoxide and carbon dioxide, and the hydrogen combines with the oxygen to produce water.

While all these changes in the substance of the candle are taking place, the candle, of course, is becoming shorter. But it is not "going" anywhere. Its materials are simply changing into other substances.

WHERE was the world before it was made?

This is a nuclear explosion. Explosions far greater than this formed the Universe.

THE WORLD

In the beginning our universe was a mass of white-hot vapours and molten materials whirling about in space. Our world was formed from this. Astronomers believe it took millions of years for the cloud to cool, contract and begin to turn into molten rock.

Modern astronomers think that many millions of years ago there was a huge explosion in space. They do not know exactly what happened. But it is possible that our sun exploded or that a much bigger companion star of the sun became a supernova—that is, it broke up violently. The debris and blazing gases from this explosion were, it is thought, flung far into space.

For more millions of years our universe boiled and bubbled. But slowly, very slowly, the fiery redness began to cool and condense into the nine planets and many more smaller bodies. All these planets now revolve around the sun.

After further vast periods of time the lava of the earth began to solidify, developing over many millions of years, into the world as we know it today.

WHERE do shadows go?

SHADOWS

Shadows need light before they can appear. If the light goes out, the shadow goes out too.

A shadow is that part of an an illuminated surface which is shielded from oncoming light rays by an object through which the light cannot pass. If the source of light is small, the outline of the shadow will be sharp and pronounced and its shape will be that of the object producing it. If the source of light is large, the shadow is very dark in the middle (the umbra) and much lighter on the outside with indistinct outlines (the penumbra).

Shadows cast by the sun always have a penumbra and the shape of the shadows cast varies with the position of the sun in the sky and the angle of its rays. An upright pole will cast a long shadow in the morning when the sun is rising but grows shorter as noon approaches. As the sun declines in the sky, the shadow grows longer again.

Human shadows have often had a mystical or magical significance. In the picture above you can see a masterly use of shadow to give form by the English painter Wright, of Derby.

WHERE was the wheel invented? WHERE is Ursa Minor?

FIRST WHEEL

The earliest wheels so 'far discovered were found in graves at Kish and Susa, two ancient Mesopotamian cities. These wheels are believed to date from 3,500 B.C. They were made from three planks, clamped together with copper clasps. This kind of wheel also existed in ancient times in Europe and the Near East. No one is sure where the wheel was invented, but this archaeological evidence suggests it was probably in ancient Mesopotamia.

A wheel with proper spokes was not invented until after 2,000 B.C. There are records of this wheel in northern Mesopotamia, central Turkey, and north-east Persia. By the 15th Century B.C., spoked wheels were being used on chariots in Syria, Egypt, and the western Mediterranean.

The solid wheel was used mostly in farming. Tripartite wheels—wheels with three spokes—were being used in the Bronze Age in Denmark, Germany, and northern Italy for carts.

The invention of the wheel made it possible for people to transport heavy objects much more easily. It also enabled them to travel farther and trade with each other more easily, and so find out about other countries and customs.

URSA MINOR

Ursa Minor is the name of a group of stars in the Northern Hemisphere. The word used in astronomy for a group of stars is "constellation".

The stars and constellations have Latin names. Ursa Minor means The Little Bear. Its brightest star is called Polaris, and is centred over the North Pole. It is of great importance in helping sailors to find their bearings when navigating at night.

Star maps of the sky will help you locate the constellations.

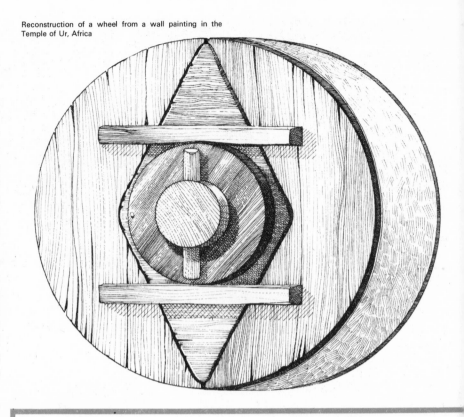

Reconstruction of a wheel from a wall painting in the Temple of Ur, Africa

THE BICYCLE

The first rideable bicycle was made by Kirkpatrick MacMillan of Dumfriesshire, Scotland, in 1839, although an attempt to construct one had been made by Jean Théson at Fontainebleau, France, in 1645.

Before this, crude machines had been made, which had no form of steering and had to be propelled by pushing the feet against the ground. Machines of this type appear on bas-reliefs in Babylon and Egypt and on frescoes in Pompeii. In England, a stained glass window, dated 1580, in the church of Stoke Poges, Buckinghamshire, shows a cherub astride such a machine.

But all these machines seem to have been four-wheeled. The true bicycle belongs to the 19th Century.

MacMillan's bicycle was driven by rods attached from pedals to a sprocket on the rear wheel. The first chain-driven bicycle was produced by Tribout and Meyer in 1869. In this year the first bicycle show—in Paris—and the first cycle road race—from Paris to Rouen—took place.

An Englishman, James Starley, of Coventry in Warwickshire, is known as "the father of the cycle industry". In 1871 he introduced a bicycle with a large driving wheel and a smaller trailing wheel. This was the "ordinary" bicycle, known to everyone as the penny-farthing. In 1874 a chain-driven bicycle with two wheels of equal diameter was designed by H. J. Lawson. This was known as the Safety bicycle and became enormously popular from about 1885 when the Rover Safety bicycle was built by John K. Starley, James's nephew.

The pneumatic tyre—in other words, a tyre filled with air—was invented in 1888 by John Boyd Dunlop, a veterinary surgeon of Belfast, Northern Ireland. By 1893 the design of the bicycle had been developed into the modern diamond frame with roller-chain drive and pneumatic-tyred wheels.

WHERE was the first bicycle made?
WHERE was the first radio signal sent from?

RADIO SIGNALS

Guglielmo Marconi is usually credited with sending the first radio message. Marconi was born in Bologna, Italy. He came to England in 1896 and obtained a British patent for his wireless telegraphy system. In 1897 he established a radio transmitter on the roof of the Post Office at St Martins-le-Grand in London, and sent a message a distance of a few hundred yards.

He continued to improve his apparatus, and in 1898 radio was installed aboard a ship at sea, the East Goodwin lightship off the south-east coast of England. In the following year wireless messages were sent across the English Channel.

The first radio transmission across the Atlantic was on December 12, 1901 from a station on the

cliffs at Poldhu, in Cornwall, and the message, three dots representing the letter S in the Morse code, was picked up at St John's in Newfoundland.

The existence of radio waves was first demonstrated by Heinrich Hertz, a German professor, in 1887. Marconi based his experiments on Hertz's research.

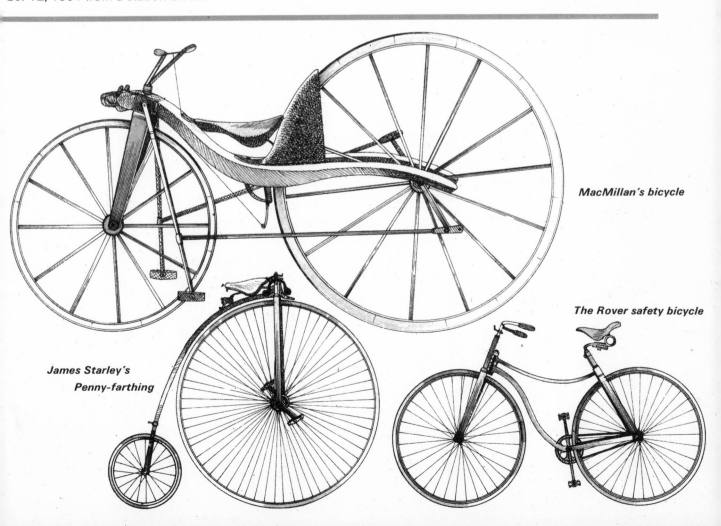

MacMillan's bicycle

The Rover safety bicycle

James Starley's
Penny-farthing

SPACE FLIGHT

On October 4, 1957, the Soviet Union launched the world's first satellite, Sputnik I, into space from a secret launching pad north of the Caspian Sea. The satellite continued to orbit the world for 92 days, ending its journey on January 4, 1958. The Russians spent 12 years developing their Sputnik.

The first manned space flight was made when Yuri Gagarin of the Soviet Union orbited the earth once in his spacecraft Vostok I in April, 1961. His journey lasted 108 minutes. He took off from Baikonur in western Siberia and landed near Engels in the Saratov region—probably close to the Sputnik's launching pad.

Man first set foot on another celestial body on July 21, 1969 when Neil Armstrong stepped on to the moon's surface. His first words were: "That's one small step for a man, one giant leap for mankind".

Below is Vostok 1 on exhibition

invented? WHERE will water not boil?
WHERE is the longest ocean cable in the world?

EARLY CLOCKS

It is believed that the Babylonians first used a pole fixed in the ground to measure the passing of time. They noticed that the position of the shadow changed during the hours of sunlight. They found that the shadow was long at sunrise and that it slowly grew shorter until it reached a point when it started to lengthen again. They noticed that at sunset the shadow was as long as it was at sunrise.

The simple shadow and pole arrangement was the basis of the various shadow clocks or sundials used by the ancient Egyptians. Eventually sundials were provided with the hour figures engraved on a metal plate.

The Egyptians also used a clepsydra or water clock. This was a basin-shaped, alabaster vessel filled with water that ran out through a hole in the bottom. The time was indicated by the level of water remaining inside.

Monks were the first to operate clocks by wheels and weights. Clocks of this type, found in monasteries, date back to the 14th Century. The first spring clock is dated about 1500.

BOILING WATER

Water will boil anywhere, but it boils at different temperatures in different places. For example, it will boil at a lower temperature up a mountain than at sea level.

The boiling point of water is the temperature at which its vapour pressure becomes equal to the outside atmospheric pressure.

As the atmospheric pressure is always changing so the boiling point of water will vary from day to day. Water boils at 100° Centigrade only when the atmospheric pressure outside is at the "standard" value.

At Quito in Ecuador, which is about 2,700 metres (or 8,800 feet) above sea level, water boils at 90° Centigrade.

People who explore in mountainous regions find a pressure-cooker very useful. The time required to cook food can be greatly reduced if the boiling point of the water is raised. The pressure-cooker does this, since it is an aluminium container fitted with a sealing ring but with a loaded pin-valve which allows steam to escape. The valve can be set at varying pressures, enabling the food to be cooked at a temperature of about 120° Centigrade.

OCEAN CABLES

The laying of the first successful transoceanic cable was completed on July 27, 1866, from Newfoundland, Canada, to Valencia Island off the south-west coast of Ireland. The cable was laid by the famous steamship Great Eastern. Since that time submarine telegraph and telephone cables have been laid all over the world.

Today the longest submarine telephone cable is the Commonwealth Pacific Cable (COMPAC).

It runs for over 9,000 miles from Australia, via Auckland, New Zealand and the Hawaiian Islands to Port Berni in western Canada. This cable was officially inaugurated on December 2, 1963. Its total cost was about £35 million.

Now that communications by satellite are being extensively used, it seems unlikely that another cable will ever be built to match COMPAC's record.

See the marine cables below

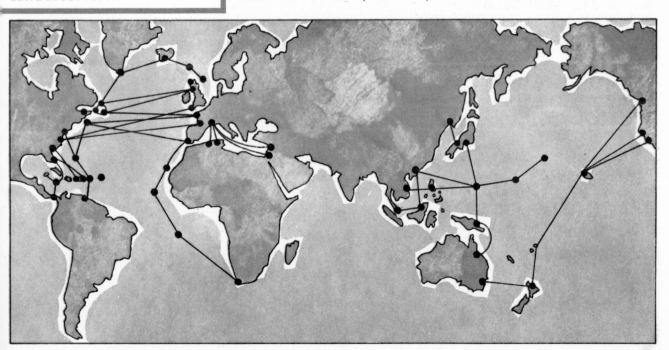

WHERE does the sun go in a total eclipse? WHERE doe
WHERE would you look for a needle beam?

TOTAL ECLIPSE

An eclipse of the sun occurs when the moon passes between the sun and the earth, thus blocking from view either the whole of the sun or part of it.

A total eclipse begins when the moon starts to move across the western side of the sun travelling towards the east. When the sun is completely covered, the beautiful halo of light surrounding it, called the corona, can be seen. This is the ring of burning gases which envelopes the main body of the sun. It is dangerous to look directly at an eclipse, since the sun's rays can burn the eyes badly.

Since the moon is far smaller than the earth it cannot block all of the earth from the sun at the same time. The moon as it sweeps across the surface of the earth blots out the sun rays only for those parts of the world in the moon's shadow.

The longest a total eclipse can last in one place on earth is seven and a half minutes. The last total eclipse of the sun occurred on June 30, 1973 and the next one will take place on July 11, 1991.

PAPER

A sheet of paper consists of vegetable fibres of different sizes, twisted and intertwined with each other and finally squeezed together to make a sheet with a surface smooth enough to write or print on.

Originally it was discovered that if a mixture of wood pulp and water was spread on a sieve, the water would drain away and leave a deposit which, when dry, could be peeled off as a sheet of paper.

Although the Chinese had been using paper since A.D. 105 it was not introduced into Europe until the 15th Century. The raw materials used for modern hand-made paper are cotton and linen rags. Such paper is very expensive to produce.

Machine-made paper is processed in paper mills from esparto grass, wood and straw, and is much cheaper. The materials for both types of paper-making have to be put through the same basic procedure of repeated washing and bleaching to get rid of impurities.

ELECTRICITY

The real answer to this question is that electricity is not stored at all. It is generated—that is, made—as it is used. Gas can be stored in huge cylinders. Electricity is produced and used immediately.

Electricity can be produced in several ways—by hydro-electric stations, which use the power of waterfalls and rivers to drive the generators; by thermal power stations, where fuel like coal and oil is used; and by nuclear power stations.

The basic method of production is the same, but the most usual source of electricity is the thermal power station. The fuel is used to heat water in the boilers to produce steam at very high pressure—up to 5,000 pounds a square inch. This steam is directed at the blades of a high-speed turbine which is connected to the generator. The generators are of two-pole construction, turning at 3,000 revolutions a minute.

These generators work on the principle of the rotation of a wire coil through a magnetic field, the application of the earliest principles discovered by pioneer scientists.

To supply this tremendous electrical energy where it is wanted, three component parts are required. First, the generating stations themselves. Second, the transmission system for transmitting large amounts of electricity to whole areas where it is needed. Third, the distribution system for distributing the power at low voltages to homes, shops and individual consumers.

So electricity is not stored. It is made, and at once used. Great skill has to be employed to keep the balance between the supply and the demand.

The current world oil shortage has made the problems of electricity production more difficult, especially in Europe and Japan.

paper come from? **WHERE** is electricity stored?

WHERE is cobalt used?

NEEDLE BEAMS

This has nothing to do with needles and nothing to do with light. A needle beam is a term used by builders and architects to describe the supports used when the foundations of a wall or a column need attention.

If a wall needs underpinning to enable the foundations to be strengthened, steel needle beams are inserted through slots cut into the wall a foot or so from the bottom. The ends of the beams are supported by screw jacks which can be moved along the beams according to the extent of the foundation area needing attention. Once the work has been done and the foundations have been restored, the needle beams are removed and the holes in the wall filled.

When a needle beam is used to shore up a column it is usually bolted on.

The needle beam is so called because it is "threaded" through the wall it has to support (see illustration).

USES OF COBALT

Can you think of any connection between a delicate Ming vase and a nuclear explosion? Difficult, isn't it? And yet there is a connection in the sense that different types of one particular substance—cobalt—have been used in the production of both.

In ancient China the beautiful blues used in the finest porcelains came from a cobalt ore. Until the early years of this century most of the world's production of cobalt went to provide colour for the porcelain and glass industries.

Today cobalt, which in its natural state is a hard silvery-white metallic substance, serves many purposes. A "cobalt bomb" can be a terrible weapon capable of distributing lethal radioactive cobalt-60 through a nuclear explosion. It can also be the means of treating certain illnesses by deep X-rays.

About a quarter of the output of cobalt goes into the making of magnets, since the metal has a high magnetic quality. It has many engineering uses. It can be employed to take away the slightly yellow tint of the iron in plate-glass windows. There is a call for it in dentistry and bone surgery.

In Australia and New Zealand ranchers were puzzled by the poor condition of sheep and cattle grazing on apparently good pasture land. Eventually it was discovered that the land did not have enough cobalt. Today small quantities of a cobalt-based compound are added either to the water supplies serving the cattle or to the land itself in the form of fertilizers.

Cobalt is also an essential food ingredient for human beings. Liver, cabbage, spinach, lettuce and watercress all contain comparatively high levels of it. About 20,000 tons of cobalt are produced every year.

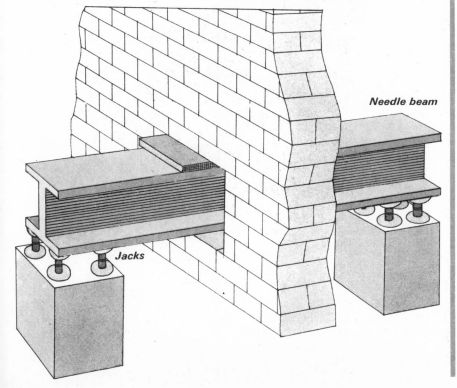

Needle beam

Jacks

ROCKETS

The rocket, as far as can be established, was invented by the Chinese during the 12th or 13th Century. The Chinese used their rockets as fireworks to mark special celebrations. A rocket has no moving parts. It is a fuel-filled container with a hole at one end where the exhaust or gases escape with such force that they propel the rocket in the direction in which it is pointed.

Rockets were used as weapons in the East until the 18th Century. Sir William Congreve added improvements in his artillery rocket, which was used in the American War of Independence and in the Napoleonic Wars. Rockets fell out of use in the 19th Century but were revived in the First World War.

Their peaceful use as line-carriers in sea rescues and as distress signals is well known. They are also used to deliver mail and to aid aeroplane take-off.

There are two categories of rocket fuel: liquid and solid. Also, rockets which are used outside the earth's atmosphere must carry their own oxygen or they would be unable to get a "burn". The space rockets carry both liquid and solid fuel. Some burn at least 1,000 pounds of fuel a second. Control of the rocket is carried out by radar and intricate design is required in directing the exhaust gases to maintain the correct flight path.

The Germans developed the rocket in the 1930s and used it in the V1 and V2 weapons which were directed at London in the Second World War.

Since then enormous advances have been made by technicians and scientists working all over the world, culminating in rockets as tall as small skyscrapers and weighing thousands of tons, which are used in the exploration of space.

weigh nothing? WHERE does sound go?
WHERE were kites first flown?

WEIGHTLESS MAN

This happens whenever the pull of gravity or the "G" factor is overcome. It can occur when an aircraft is put into a steep dive.

Astronauts experience this "weightlessness" in space. So that they can get used to its effects before leaving the earth's atmosphere, special machines have been built in an attempt to create the same conditions. Astronauts also train for space weightlessness in large water tanks.

It is essential that an astronaut should get used to the feeling of weightlessness which occurs when earth's gravity is no longer effective. For instance, he cannot pour liquid into a cup or drink from it. With enough practice, however, he can learn to move about, eat, drink and sleep without difficulty.

When an astronaut goes outside his vehicle in space, there is some gravitational pull between him and his cabin. But owing to the small mass of both, the attraction between them is negligible. It is far too small to bring him back if he jumped off. So he has to use a special life-line to prevent himself from drifting into space.

SOUND

The simple answer, of course, is that the sounds you hear go into your brain by way of your ears. But what is sound?

When you are listening to pop music, you are at the receiving end of sounds. But what is going on at the sending end? The players are making vibrations on their instruments and sending sound waves through the air to you. The point to remember is that sound waves must have something to carry them. Usually this is air, but it can also be water or the earth under your feet, both of which are better sound wave conductors than air.

The Indians of North America used to put their ears to the ground to hear the sound of their enemies' horses, when the air gave them no warning. But in a vacuum no sound can be heard. The loudest pop music, if it could be played in a vacuum, would make no noise.

The question "Where does sound go?" can be put another way—"When does sound stop?". The answer to this one is that sound stops when the vibrations sending out the sound waves come to a standstill.

FIRST KITES

Kites have been used in Asia since time immemorial. Some evidence dates their invention at around 1,000 B.C. Kite flying has been a national pastime for many centuries among the Chinese, Japanese, Koreans and Malayans. Kites held great religious significance in Asia, as they were believed to keep evil spirits away when flown at night.

But there is also a tradition that they were invented nearly four centuries before Christ by Archytas of Tarentum, in southern Italy. He was a Greek philosopher and scientist, and a friend of Plato, the great philosopher.

Kite flying strictly for pleasure has many supporters in China, where the ninth day of the ninth month is designated Kite Day.

Kites have often been used in simple bridge building by attaching a cable to the kite and flying it across the river or gap. In meteorology kites have been used to carry weather recording instruments aloft.

The current kite flying record of four and a half miles was achieved with a string of 10 kites. The total surface of the 10 kites was 683 square feet. The line used for this record-breaking flight was more than nine miles long.

WHERE would you find the Garden of Eden? WHERE is the

General Knowledge

WAILING WALL

The Wailing Wall is in Jerusalem. It consists of the surviving portion of the temple built by the Jews on the site of King Solomon's temple. The temple was destroyed in A.D. 70 by the Roman Emperor Titus to punish the rebellious Jews. For centuries the Jews have bewailed the loss of their temple at the western or Wailing Wall.

Jerusalem was divided after the Second World War but Jewish forces regained control of the Old City, which contains the Wailing Wall, in the Six-Day War of 1967.

GARDEN OF EDEN

The short answer is that you would not find it. The Garden of Eden is the place where God is supposed to have created a garden for Adam, the first man. Some people hold it to have been situated in the Mesopotamian region between the Rivers Tigris and Euphrates. The Tree of Knowledge grew in this garden and it was there that man fell from grace in God's eyes because, at the prompting of Eve, the first woman, he ate fruit from this tree.

Because of this act of disobedience, it is said, God devised three punishments. The man was to till the earth, which was cursed; the woman was to experience painful childbirth; and the serpent who prompted the woman to persuade the man to eat the fruit was from that day forth to be hated by mankind. Adam had to be driven out of the Garden of Eden because the Tree of Life also grew there and this would have endowed him with immortality. The inference is that man chose knowledge and death rather than ignorance and eternal life.

The Garden of Eden has been portrayed in many famous paintings and poems. In man's imagination it has always been an ideal to which he longs to return.

Vailing Wall? **WHERE** would you find the Hesperides?
WHERE would you find Davy Jones's locker?

THE HESPERIDES

The Hesperides, in Greek mythology, were the maidens who guarded the tree that bore the golden apples given by Mother Earth to the goddess Hera, when she married Zeus. Another version of the myth says the maidens were the daughters of Erelius and Night. Their names are usually given as Aegle, Erytheia and Hesperis, and they lived in Arcadia, which was thought of as a sort of ideal Garden of Eden. Modern Arcadia is in central Greece.

DAVY JONES'S LOCKER

For several centuries men and ships lost at sea have been said to go to Davy Jones's Locker. Davy Jones is the spirit of the sea—the sailors' devil—and his locker is the ocean. A character in *Sir Launcelot Greaves*, a novel by Tobias George Smollett (1721–71) observes: "I have seen Davy Jones in the shape of a blue flame, d'ye see, hopping to and from on the spritsail yardarm".

In 1803 the *Naval Chronicles* stated: "The . . . seaman would have met a watery grave; or, to use a seaman's phrase, gone to Davy Jones's locker." In Chamier's *Saucy Arethusa*, written in 1837, we find: "The boat was capsized . . . and . . . all hands are snug enough in Davy Jones's locker."

There have been many explanations as to how Davy Jones came to stand for the sailors' devil. One is that the name Jones evolved from Jonah, the Old Testament prophet, who ended up in the belly of a whale. If that is so, why Davy? For Davy seems to be an essential part of the title as shown by variations—David Jones, Old Davy and, simply, Davy. Another suggestion is that, as Jonah became the Welsh name Jones, a popular Welsh Christian name was added.

ERCOLE ALL'ESPERIDI

WHERE is the Mona Lisa?   WHERE is the Alhambra?

MONA LISA

The world's most famous portrait, painted by Leonardo da Vinci (1452–1519) between 1503 and 1506, hangs today in the Louvre in Paris. The Louvre, formerly a palace of the French kings, is now a museum of art and antiquities which is beyond all valuation.

The Mona Lisa is also called La Gioconda because the sitter's married name was Giocondo. It has been in France from the day in 1516 when Leonardo left Italy to settle there—except for two occasions. Once, in 1911, the picture was stolen from the Louvre and found two years later in Italy. The second time it left France for 26 days, on a fantastically well-guarded and highly insured visit to the United States as a guest of President John F. Kennedy.

Leonardo da Vinci began painting Lisa when she was 24 and he was 51. She used to come to the great master's studio in the late afternoon when the light was soft. Over the three years, Leonardo became fascinated by his model, and perhaps that was the reason why her husband, Francesco del Giocondo, never received the finished portrait. The artist always made the excuse that he had not quite finished it. He carried it with him wherever he went—to Milan, to Rome and, finally, to France where King Francis I offered the artist a palace in the beautiful Loire valley, the Chateau de Cloux.

It is believed that Francis I paid 4,000 gold crowns for the Mona Lisa, but it was not until after Leonardo's death that the king was able, at last, to possess the painting of the Florentine lady with the enigmatic smile. Thereafter, it remained in the possession of the kings and emperors of France. The picture hung at Fontainebleau, at Versailles and at the Tuileries. There in 1800 it hung on the wall of Napoleon Bonaparte's bedroom!

THE ALHAMBRA

The Alhambra is a palace and fortress at Granada, in Spain, overlooking the River Darro. It was built by the Moors who occupied Spain in the Middle Ages. The Moors were the inhabitants of Mauretania, an African province of the Roman Empire, which we know today as Morocco. The Alhambra was begun in 1248 and completed in 1354. Its name comes from the Arabic *qal'at al hamra* (the red castle) and was given to the building because of the red brick of the outer walls.

Today only some splendid remnants of its former glory are to be seen, for in the 16th Century Charles V had much of it rebuilt or replaced. Over the outer arch of the Gate of Judgment is carved an open hand, and legend said that the fortress would never be captured until the hand grasped the key sculptured on the inner arch.

The largest room is the Hall of the Ambassadors and the most romantic the Hall of the Abencerrages, which is called after a famous Moorish family who settled in Spain in the 8th Century. According to legend, 36 knights of the Abencerrages family were massacred in the hall of Boabdil, the last Moorish King of Granada, who died about 1495.

WHERE is the world's largest painting? WHERE did cricke

WHERE is radium found?

LARGEST PAINTING

The largest painting ever made was undoubtedly *Panorama of the Mississippi*, completed by the American John Banvard in 1846.

The painting depicted the great river over its 1,200 miles course, on a strip some 5,000 feet long and 12 feet wide. In area it was nearly as big as a field of an acre and a half—an amazing size.

But this painting was destroyed when the barn on Long Island, New York, where it was stored burned down in 1891.

The largest painting now in existence is *The Battle of Gettysburg*, completed in 1883 after two-and-a-half years' work. It took Paul Philippoteaus of France and 16 assistants to paint the 410-foot-long picture. It is 70 feet high and weighs nearly five-and-a-half tons. The painting is now in a private collection in Winston-Salem, North Carolina, United States. Size alone, of course, is no guide to quality.

CRICKET

Pictures belonging to the middle of the 13th Century show a simple team game with bat and ball which bears a marked resemblance to cricket, the national game of England. The first written evidence about the game is possibly to be found in an extract from the accounts of King Edward I of England in 1300. This refers to some money which was spent by the young Prince Edward on a game called "creag".

Cricket was being played by boys of the free school of Guildford, Surrey, in 1550. Oliver Cromwell, Lord Protector of England, was said to have played both cricket and football in his youth, and a kind of cricket club at St Albans, Hertfordshire, was mentioned in 1666. The first regular cricket club was formed in the Hampshire village of Hambledon in 1750.

The game has been played under recognized rules at least since the beginning of the 18th Century. The first definite match recorded was played in 1679 in Sussex—11 a side and for a stake of 50 guineas. In 1719 the "Londoners" met the "Kentish men" in what must have been the first match at county level.

At first the greatest enthusiasm for the game was in the southern counties. The most famous cricket centre was the Artillery Ground, Finsbury. Here was played on June 18, 1744, the famous match between Kent and All England. This was the first game to be recorded in A. Haygarth's *Scores and Biographies 1744–1878*.

The Marylebone Cricket Club, which eventually became the game's ruling authority, was established in 1787. In 1814 it purchased its present ground at St. John's Wood, London, named after the club's founder, Thomas Lord.

Cricket is now widely played in the English-speaking lands.

begin?   **WHERE** is Britain's money made?
WHERE does the word "barbecue" come from?

RADIUM

Radium is found in the ore of uranium. Two French scientists working in Paris discovered radium in 1890. Professor and Mme. Curie found this rare and precious element in a mineral called pitch-blende, a black substance which also contains uranium. During a period of four years they treated six tons of this material and obtained a teaspoonful of a pure radioactive substance which they called radium.

They found that radium had many very unusual properties. It affected ordinary photographic plates, it made certain substances glow when placed in the dark, and it quickly killed off tiny dangerous organisms when placed near them.

Radium gives off powerful radioactive waves—the well-known gamma rays. These are used in the treatment of various diseases, especially in the case of cancer where "deep ray" treatment is given.

Pierre and Marie Curie were awarded the Nobel Prize for physics for their work. Professor Curie was killed in a motor accident in 1906, but Mme. Curie continued the work they had started together and in 1911 was awarded the Nobel Prize for Chemistry.

BARBECUE

The word "barbecue" comes from the Spanish word "barbacoa". Barbacoa was the native Haitian name adopted by the Spanish for a kind of scaffolding. Then the French used it to describe a sort of grid or grill—one, no doubt, often used for cooking. The word came to designate an animal roasted whole, usually out of doors.

In the 19th Century, Americans adopted the name barbacoa and anglicized it to barbecue, which came to mean an open air feast or social gathering, as we know it today.

BRITAIN'S MONEY

Britain's money is made in the Royal Mint on Tower Hill, in London. The word "mint" is used to describe a place where coins are manufactured, usually with the authority of the state.

Gold, Silver and base metal coins were being used by various tribes in Britain before the Roman occupation. In the 3rd Century the Emperor Marcus Aurelius Carausius opened three English mints, one of which was in London. These were soon closed however, and not until the 6th Century was there further definite record of a mint in England.

Seventy mints were in existence in England at the time William the Conqueror landed because the transport of money from one place to another was so risky. As conditions improved, the number of mints declined. Since the 16th Century, all English gold and silver coins, with one or two important exceptions, such as the Great Recoinage of 1696 to 1698, have been struck in the London Mint.

To enable decimal coinage to be produced without interrupting current output, it was announced in 1967 that a mint would open in Llantrisant, South Wales. Queen Elizabeth II struck the first decimal coin on December 17, 1968, when, accompanied by the Duke of Edinburgh and the Prince of Wales, she opened the new mint. It is expected that the South Wales mint will take over coin production in Britain in 1975.

WHERE does velvet come from?   WHERE is the Whispering

VELVET

Velvet comes from silk, but there are many imitations made from cotton and other materials. Real velvet is a closely woven fabric made by weaving loops of silk on to two silk backcloths, one on top of the other. In between the two backcloths the woven silk will form what is called a pile. The pile is the soft, furry hairs characteristic of velvet and many carpets.

The two layers of silk, which have been woven face-to-face, will have long furry pile yarns connecting the two layers. After the cloth is woven, the two layers are sliced apart leaving two separate soft rows of velvet.

Velvet was originally developed in the 15th Century in Italy from where the art spread throughout the world. Turkish velvets were especially successful, and beautiful designs from 16th and 17th Century Turkey survive today.

THE CALENDAR

Early in history man began counting time by days, months and seasons and so had the beginnings of a calendar. When he studied the supposed movement of the sun more closely he began to use the year as a unit of time.

The Greeks dated everything from the Olympic Register, a traditional list of the victors in the Olympic games starting in 776 B.C. The Romans counted time from the founding of their city in 753 B.C. The Mohammedans use the Hejira, or flight of Mohammed from Mecca, A.D. 622. Jewish reckoning dates back to the Creation, calculated as having taken place 3,760 years and three months before Christ's birth-date. The Christian practice of dating events from the birth of Christ did not come into general use until the time of Charlemagne (9th Century), and a mistake was made

WHISPERING GALLERY

The Whispering Gallery is one of the most famous features of Sir Christopher Wren's great masterpiece, St Paul's Cathedral in London.

If you speak in this gallery, which runs round the inside of the great dome, the sound waves of your voice will be carried round to the opposite side of the gallery because the waves are prevented from going outwards by the stones lining the circular wall.

The great dome of St Paul's is really two domes—an outer dome with a diameter of 148 feet and an inner dome with a diameter of 103 feet. A hollow cone of brickwork between them supports a steeple-like structure in six diminishing stages culminating in the ball and cross. The top of the cross is 404 feet above the ground.

St Paul's has been acclaimed as the most magnificent domed build-

which placed the Christ's birth five years too late.

In 46 B.C., acting on the advice of the astronomer Sosigenes, Julius Caesar fixed the year at $365\frac{1}{4}$ days, giving every fourth year, or leap year, an extra day. But the correction by a whole day every four years was too much, and by the 16th Century the Julian calendar was 13 days behind the solar year.

In 1582, Pope Gregory XIII directed that 10 days should be dropped from the calendar. He also directed that three times in every 400 years the leap year arrangement should be omitted, by not counting as leap years the years ending in two noughts unless they are divisible by 400. This arrangement will keep the calendar and solar year together until the year 5,000, when the difference will be one day.

ing of the Renaissance period. It replaced the Norman cathedral which was destroyed in the Great Fire of London in 1666 and whose tower and spire were 124 feet higher than the present building.

The foundation stone of the new St Paul's was laid in 1675 and 35 years later the final stone of the cupola was put into position.

Great craftsmen were employed on the interior decoration. Francis Bird carved the Conversion of St Paul over the great pediment. Grinling Gibbons, one of England's and the world's finest woodcarvers, worked on the choir stalls, and the wrought iron work was done by Jean Tijou, the renowned ironsmith.

During the Second World War St Paul's was hit three times by bombs, the most serious damage being the destruction of the high altar on the night of October 10, 1940. The new high altar was dedicated as a British Commonwealth war memorial in May, 1958.

The tombs of many famous men—Nelson, Wellington, Roberts, Jellicoe and Beatty—are either in the cathedral or in the crypt beneath. Wren, too, is buried there, and his epitaph is inscribed in Latin over the north door. It is *Si monumentum requiris, circumspice*—If you seek his memorial, look around you.

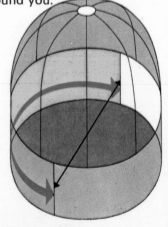

The red arrow shows how sound travels around the walls

Gallery?   **WHERE** did calendars begin?

WHERE does America keep her gold? WHERE is the Littl

WHERE were knives and forks first used? WHERE wou

LITTLE MERMAID

The famous bronze statue of the Little Mermaid, carved by Edvard Eriksen, is posed on a rock near the Langelinie promenade in Copenhagen harbour, Denmark. She is the heroine of Hans Christian Andersen's fairy tale about a mermaid who falls in love with a prince and who sacrifices her tongue to exchange her fish-tail for human legs.

Hans Christian Andersen (1805–75) was born in Odense, Denmark. When he was 14, he went to Copenhagen to try to be an actor or opera singer. He was not successful and turned to writing, but failed in that, too. However, a friend who had faith in his talent persuaded the King of Denmark to grant him a pension, so that he could continue his education and travel to other countries. Soon afterwards he began to write poems, plays, novels and travel books that sold well.

Nowadays these are all forgotten, and the world remembers him for his fairy tales which appeared in 1835. Today they are published in more than 60 languages.

AMERICA'S GOLD

America keeps most of her gold at Fort Knox, a United States Army reservation, about 35 miles south of Louisville in Kentucky. Covering 110,000 acres, the reservation contains the United States Army Armoured Centre and the principal United States bullion depository.

The fort was established in 1918 as Camp Knox and was used as the army's Field Artillery officer training school. In 1932 the name was changed, and the following year the 1st Cavalry Regiment was moved from Texas to Fort Knox, where it was mechanized.

For maximum security, the bullion depository was built at Fort Knox in 1936. By the second half of the 20th Century the gold stocks there were valued at more than 10,000 million dollars. The gold is housed in a solid square bomb-proof building constructed of granite, steel and concrete, enclosing a two-level torch-proof steel and concrete vault. Added security is provided by guards, sentries and an encircling steel fence, as well as by mechanical protective devices, such as the photo-electric eye.

During the Second World War the gold vault was used as a storage place for the original copy of the United States constitution, the Declaration of Independence and England's Magna Carta.

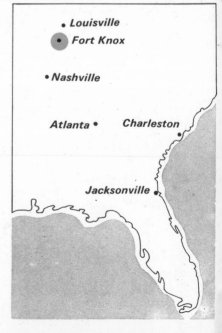

Mermaid? WHERE would you use a rouble, yen, rupee, you look for a yard of ale? drachma, guilder?

ROUBLE, YEN, RUPEE, DRACHMA, GUILDER

You would use a rouble in the Soviet Union, a yen in Japan, a rupee in India and Pakistan, a drachma in Greece, and a guilder in Holland. They are all units of the monetary systems of those countries.

The rouble, which is divided into 100 kopeks, was the name for silver bar money which was in use in Russia from the 14th to the 17th Centuries. Peter the Great set up the modern system of coins, and the silver bar money was abolished.

The yen was originally a gold coin, but was changed to silver. A one yen coin is now made of aluminium and the five and ten yen pieces are made of nickel.

The word rupee means "silver coin". It came into use in 1542 when the Sultan of Delhi, Sher Sha, reorganized the currency. It was kept as a monetary unit and is now divided into 100 noye paise (new paisas). Large amounts of rupees have special names: a lakh is 100,000 and a crore is ten million rupees.

The drachma, in Ancient Greece was a silver coin and also a measure of weight. There were 100 drachmae to one mina which weighed about one pound. The modern drachma is divided into 100 lepta.

The guilder, which is the currency of The Netherlands and its overseas territories, is divided into 100 cents. This unit of currency spread to Northern Europe from Florence in Italy and is also used under the name of florin.

KNIVES AND FORKS

Knives were invented a long time before forks. Flint knives for general purposes were used in the Stone Age. The Romans had eating knives. But even in the 16th Century only very rich houses had enough knives for each guest at dinner to have one to himself. This meant that people often carried their own knives with them in a sheath round their waists. Often they were made in pairs so that even before forks were employed you did not have to use your fingers.

The first forks had only two prongs like a carving fork, and there was usually only one in a house. The use of forks at table was probably introduced into Europe from the East through the Venetians in the 11th Century.

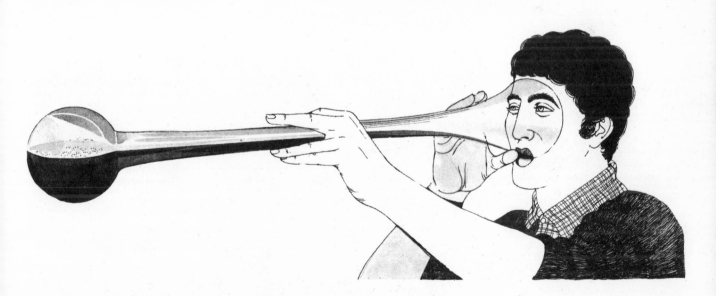

YARD OF ALE

You would look for, and perhaps find, a yard of ale in an old public house or a tavern in England. It is a narrow tube, three feet long, opening out at one end and with a bulb at the other. When filled with ale or beer, it forms one yard of ale. Although now rare, these strange-shaped glasses can still be found hanging on the walls of inns, particularly old or historic ones, as a curiosity.

This odd drinking vessel was an example of the glass-blower's art. But it was never in general use for drinking. Instead it was used either as a joke or as a challenge. When the glass was filled to the brim with ale or beer, the contestant had to drink "the yard" without pausing or taking breath. At a really lively party, every man present would have had to take his turn. When this type of entertainment was popular, the locally brewed ale was probably less strong and intoxicating than it is now. But the feat still required considerable swallowing power and breath control.

WHERE did rugby football begin? WHERE is the highest
WHERE is Constable country?

RUGBY

The highly organized rugby football games of today developed from the crowd game of ancient and medieval Britain in which a round or oval object—usually the inflated bladder of an animal—was kicked, punched or driven towards a goal. The origins of games between two teams, which attempt to kick, carry or otherwise force a ball through a goal or across a goal line defended by their opponents, are lost in antiquity.

When football was taken up by the great English public schools, all agreed that the ball must never be carried or passed by hand in the direction of the opponents' goal. It was a violation of this rule by William Webb Ellis at Rugby School in 1823 which led to the division of modern footballers into those who want to play only with their feet and those who wish to use both feet and hands.

At first, Ellis's behaviour was condemned even at Rugby. But the school soon decided to permit running with the ball by players who received it by a fair catch. Then it was permitted if the ball was caught on the bound. Later other restrictions on running with it were abolished.

Ellis became a great hero and a tablet on one of the boundary walls of Rugby School bears this inscription: "This stone commemorates the exploit of William Webb Ellis who with a fine disregard for the rules of football as played in his time took the ball in his arms and ran with it, thus originating the distinctive feature of the Rugby game. A.D. 1823".

It was some time before rugby football was accepted as a game in its own right, but on January 26, 1871 representatives of 17 clubs and three schools met at the Pall Mall restaurant, Regent Street, London. They formed the Rugby

HIGHEST RAILWAY

The highest railway in the world is in Peru. A branch siding of the track rises to 15,844 feet above sea-level. But the highest point on the main line is 15,688 feet in a tunnel called La Galera.

All the railway lines in Peru belonging to the Central Railway of Peru are of standard gauge (4 feet 8½ inches), like most railways in Europe and North America.

The highest railway station in the world is also in Peru, at La Galera. This station is at an altitude of 15,685 feet above sea-level. Henry Deiggs was the engineer for this extraordinary railway line, which was completed nearly a hundred years ago.

Football Union, drafted by-laws, appointed officers and instructed a committee of 13 to draw up the basis of the code in use at Rugby School.

railway in the world?
WHERE does the blue in blue cheese come from?

Detail from "Dedham Vale" by John Constable

BLUE CHEESE

Blue cheeses are all made from cows' milk except for the famous French Roquefort cheese, which comes from ewes' milk.

The blue in blue cheeses is essentially blue mould. But it is extremely good for you. What happens is that an organism similar to penicillin is added to the milk or curd used to make ordinary white cheese. The mould, during three to six months of ripening, grows either in small, irregular, natural openings in the cheese or in machine-made perforations, depending on the type of cheese

The small amounts of mould reproduce or spread to give the typical blue streaks in the white cheese, and, once ripened, the distinctive flavour. Blue cheeses are usually heavily salted to add to the flavour.

CONSTABLE COUNTRY

The neighbourhood of Dedham, in Essex, and Flatford, in Suffolk, England, is often spoken of as "Constable country" because it provided so many subjects for the brush of John Constable (1776–1837), the English landscape painter.

This picture is "Dedham Vale".

It has been said that Constable was the first artist to discover that trees were green. What this really means is that, in the days when Constable began to paint, it was fashionable to represent trees and fields in pictures in a dull brown colour which was considered "harmonious" and also to re-design the landscape to make it more majestic or romantic.

Constable had no use for such notions. He depicted the beauty of the English scene, with its changing seasons, as he saw it. So it was a long time before he was recognized as a great painter. When he tried to reproduce the effect of shimmering light on trees the critics talked contemptuously of "Constable's snow". They thought his use of green vulgar and showy.

However, in 1824 three of his landscapes which he sent for exhibition at the Paris Salon were awarded a gold medal and had considerable influence.

WHERE are the Elysian Fields? **WHERE** was the first book

ELYSIAN FIELDS

The Elysian Fields was a phrase used in Greek mythology to describe what we would call Heaven. Before European navigators sailed far beyond the Mediterranean and found other lands inhabited with people like themselves, people believed the world was flat. In early Greek mythology the souls of those who died went for refuge to the Infernal Regions. This the "afterworld" was said to lie at the extremity of the earth.

At that extremity were the Elysian Fields or the Isles of the Blest. It is thought by some that this land adorned with every beauty might well be the Canary Islands or the Azores in the Atlantic Ocean.

Later when the Greeks learned more of other lands, they changed the location of the Infernal Regions to the centre of the earth. There were two great regions in the Underworld. One was the Elysian Fields, where those who had led a just life in the world above ground joined the children and favourites of the gods of Olympus and where harsh weather was never known and soft breezes forever refreshed the beautiful land.

The other place was Tartarus, the awful region of the damned, who had committed crimes against the gods and were punished by tortures. One inmate was Tantalus, son of Zeus, the father of the gods. He had betrayed his father's secrets and was condemned to stand forever with water all around him and rich fruit just above his head. When he tried to eat and drink, both fruit and water drew away from him.

From this story we get the word "tantalize". Another prisoner was Ixion, father of the Centaurs, who was bound to a rolling, flaming wheel for the rest of time for attempting to win the love of Hera, sister and wife of Zeus.

FIRST PRINTED BOOK

The first known book to be printed from movable type was the Bible, probably in the year 1455. It was certainly on sale by the middle of the year 1456. The book was printed at Mainz in Germany. It is often called the Gutenberg Bible, from the name of the man who is generally supposed to have been the printer, although two other men called Fust and Schoeffer are also associated with the task.

Sometimes this Bible is called The Forty-two Line Bible, because it had forty-two lines to the page.

Another name for it is the Mazarin Bible, because a copy was discovered in the Mazarin Library in Paris in the year 1760. A copy of the first volume, in fine condition and with the old binding still on it, was sold for £21,000 at an auction in London in 1947.

The first Bible to be printed in Ireland in 1716 made an error in the Gospel of St John, chapter 5, verse 14. The text should read "Sin no more", but the printer put "Sin *on* more". A much more costly mistake—for the printers—

rinted? WHERE is the Bridge of Sighs?
WHERE is the quarter-deck of a ship?

BRIDGE OF SIGHS

The Bridge of Sighs (*Ponte dei Sospiri*) is in Venice and connects the east side of the Doge's Palace with the old state prisons, crossing the Rio di Palazzo. Its name symbolizes the sadness of the prisoners crossing the bridge. The Doge's Palace was begun early in the 14th Century and took several centuries to complete. The Bridge was not built until the 17th Century. It became the path by which prisoners crossed to the "*pozzi*", the prisons on the other side of the canal.

The Bridge of Sighs is one of nearly 400 bridges over some 150 canals which make up the thoroughfares of Venice, a city built on wooden piles driven into the mud of the lagoon. The city became known as the "Mistress of the Adriatic" from the custom carried out each year by the city's rulers, from the 12th to the 18th Century, of throwing a wedding ring into the Adriatic in token of their claim to dominion over that sea.

Lord Byron's famous reference to the Bridge of Sighs appears in his poem, *Childe Harold's Pilgrimage:*
"I stood in Venice, on the Bridge
   of Sighs;
"A palace and a prison on each
   hand".

was made in the reign of Charles I. Psalm 44 says: "The fool hath said in his heart, there is no God". But the printer made it read: "The fool hath said in his heart, there is a God". That little slip was punished with a fine of £3,000 and the destruction of all the copies—proving it pays to be careful!

In book-printing history the name of the Englishman William Caxton, called the Father of English Printing, will always be remembered. He set up his press in 1476 close to Westminster Abbey.

QUARTER-DECK

The quarter-deck, as its name implies, is only part of a deck. In a sailing vessel it is that portion of the upper deck between the main-mast and the stern or back of the ship. The upper deck is the highest complete deck having all openings fitted with permanent means for closure against sea and weather.

In naval vessels the quarter-deck is that most glamorous part of the ship, an area of the weather deck—the highest continuous deck exposed to the weather—reserved for the officers of the ship.

Ships' decks serve the same purpose as floors and roofs in a building. They provide living and working surfaces, add strength to the structure of a ship and form a cover to keep bad weather out. Decks may be given numbers or letters to distinguish them from each other, but those which serve a definite purpose have their own distinctive names.

In the British Navy officers are allowed to drink the loyal toast seated since in the old days the deck "ceilings" were so low.

would you find the Rose of Sharon?

ROSE OF SHARON

You would find the most famous reference to the rose of Sharon in the Bible. It is chapter 2, verse 1 of the Song of Solomon, the 22nd book of the Old Testament—"I am the rose of Sharon, and the lily of the valleys".

The rose of Sharon is a low bushy plant which originated in the Mediterranean region but is naturalized in Britain and other north European countries. Known also by the name of Aaron's beard, it has evergreen leaves and yellow flowers, and is a member of the St John's wort family.

There are more than 300 species of this family which has a wide distribution in most temperate and tropical countries of the world. Forty species are to be found in the United States, where some are specially cultivated for their bright, showy flowers.

Ever since the plant was immortalised in the "Song of Solomon" it has become a synonym for grace and elegance. The flower is by no means spectacular but it has a shy and delicate quality.

UNCLE SAM

It is thought that the original Uncle Sam was an affable, pleasant man named Samuel Wilson (1766–1854), who lived in Troy, New York State, and supplied beef to the United States Army in the war with Britain in 1812. Wilson was known locally as "Uncle Sam" and, as government purchasers stamped U.S. on the barrels of meat being shipped, local workmen referred to it as "Uncle Sam's beef".

Tradition has it that the name was picked up by soldiers and soon came into familiar usage as a nickname for the United States. A resolution passed by the Congress of the United States in 1961 recognized Wilson as the namesake of the national symbol.

The symbolic Uncle Sam is a tall, thin, angular figure with long white hair and chin whiskers. He is usually dressed in a swallowtailed coat, waistcoat, top hat and striped trousers. In American stories and tales he is associated with Yankee Doodle, the British-inspired nickname for American colonials during the American Revolution, and with Brother Jonathan, a country folk-hero who always beats his enemies by surprising displays of native intelligence and wit.

Uncle Sam live? **WHERE** are the world's earliest paintings?

These delicately drawn deer are on the wall of a cave in Lascaux, France. They have a startlingly "modern" look.

EARLIEST PAINTINGS

The earliest paintings of which we have records are on the walls of caves in France and Spain. They are paintings of animals, mostly of horses, bulls and bison.

Those in France are at a place called Lascaux, in the Dordogne area. They are painted in thick black outline. Some of the bodies are filled in with red or brown paint. On the edge of the roof of the cave is a frieze of horses and bulls. It looks as though the cave people were trying to decorate the roof of the cave to a pattern.

Other famous early paintings are at a place called Altamira, in the province of Santander, Spain. Here the walls of the cave are covered with standing and squatting bison, thickly outlined in black and filled in with red.

The people who did the paintings took a lot of trouble to mix the colours properly. The black they used came from soot, and the red and yellow from iron. They stored the colours in bones and skulls, and mixed them with water, then put the paint on the walls with their fingers or brushes.

Some of the paintings were not purely for decoration. At Lascaux there are drawings of oxen and goats about to fall into a pit. Probably the people thought that if they painted the animals they wanted to kill on their cave walls, they would catch them more easily.

The name given to the cave art of this period is palaeolithic art.

WHERE was Valhalla? WHERE is the 'lost continent'?

VALHALLA

In ancient legends about the Norsemen, Valhalla was the place where all the brave warriors went when they died.

The kind of man they most admired was one who had great courage and a spirit of adventure. The warriors who went to Valhalla were supposed to lead a very happy life, eating boar's meat daily and amusing themselves by fighting each other. They were supposed to live in Valhalla till Doomsday, the end of the world. Then, led by Odin, father of the gods, they would march out of the 640 doors of the palace to fight against the giants.

LOST CONTINENT

The lost continent is a legendary island called Atlantis. It was discribed by Plato, a philosopher who lived in ancient Greece, as being in the Atlantic and also as being larger than Asia Minor and Libya put together! The Greek legends claimed that Atlantis had been inhabited by a powerful nation who had offended the gods by their independence and disrespect. The gods took their revenge. Some versions of the story say that it was submerged and others that it was destroyed by an earthquake about 9,000 B.C.

Some people have tried to identify Atlantis with America, some with Scandinavia, the Canaries and even the Palestine region. Many naturalists and philosophers, including Buffon, Montaigne and Voltaire, have theorized about Atlantis. Attempts have been made to prove that the Basques of Spain and France, the original inhabitants of Italy and the Indians of South America were descended from the Atlanteans, who were said to have overrun the entire Mediterranean.

One theory is that the Minoan civilisation was destroyed by the eruption of a volcano on Thera (Santorin) — or "lost Atlantis". Thera's cliffs are shown below.

WHERE is the Winter Palace?
WHERE was the first stamp used?

WINTER PALACE

The Winter Palace is in Leningrad in the Soviet Union. It was built between 1754 and 1761 by the Empress Elizabeth, daughter of Peter the Great. The architect of the palace was Rastrelli and the proportions of the building are so good that its huge size is not immediately apparent.

Leningrad, then called St Petersburg, was the capital of the Russian Empire from 1703 to 1917, when the capital was moved to Moscow. It is the second largest city in the Soviet Union and was built by Peter the Great,

against his ministers' advice, on unsuitable terrain and with a terrifying death toll in building labourers. The site at the mouth of the River Neva was marshy. Its great advantage was that it was a vital link with Europe and Russia's only outlet to the Baltic.

The design of the city is magnificent. Its contacts with Europe brought its citizens more freedom of thought. The first blood of the Russian Revolution was shed outside the walls of the Winter Palace, a fact which gives it great symbolic importance to the Russian workers.

FIRST STAMP

The first postage "label" or stamp was used in England in May, 1840. Letters had been sent by post since the time of the Egyptians. The Greeks, Romans, Chinese and Arabs all used pigeon-post very effectively. They sent a duplicate letter by a different pigeon in case the first bird met a hawk on the way.

Before this first stamp—the Penny Black of 1840—many marks had been used in Britain to record time and place of receipt, and money paid or owed. Rowland Hill started a movement for Post Office reform. This was founded on pre-payment for letters and a standard charge of one penny, regardless of distance. The idea of a sticky stamp was suggested to Hill by Charles Knight. The design was taken from a medallion showing the head of Queen Victoria, designed by William Wyon.

These first stamps were printed in sheets of 240. Perforations had not been invented, and the first job of the day for post office clerks was to cut rows of stamps out of the sheets. They were backed with what was called "cement" and many people found that they were difficult to stick on their letters.

These Penny Black stamps were in use for 11 months. Of the 68 million printed, six million still survive. They are not rare but collectors like to have a good example of the first stamp issued.

The rarest stamp in the world was in fact issued 16 years later. This is the British Guiana one cent which was discovered in 1873 by a schoolboy who sold it for six shillings. In 1922 it fetched £7,343.

Collectors today make a point of looking for stamps that have been misprinted, since as these, being rarer, have a great deal more value. A common misprint is for the perforation to be omitted.

WHERE was Expo '70?   WHERE do you find pygmies?

EXPO 70

Expo 70 took place in Osaka, Japan. It was the first world fair to be held on the Asian continent and commemorated the 100th anniversary of the coming of modern Western civilization to Japan. Expo 70 attracted more visitors than any previous world fair. From March 15 to September 13 in 1970 it was visited by more than 64 million people.

Seventy-six nations plus the United Nations Organization took part. The United States built an extraordinary building, elliptical in shape, made out of plastic and supported by air. The Soviet Union built a pavilion to rise like a sharp-edged arrow on top of which shone a huge red star which could be seen for miles around.

The fair also had the 1,100-foot Expo Tower from which the visitors could enjoy a spectacular view of the Kita Settsu mountains to the north-west, and to the south-west a rather less beautiful sight—industrial Osaka.

Six of the buildings have been preserved since the close of the fair, including the splendid Japanese garden which covers over 60 acres.

PYGMIES

The best-known pygmies are a people known as the Bambuti, who live in the African republic of the Congo. They are nomadic hunters and eat wild plants. They seldom stay in any one place for longer than a month, during which time they live in simple huts made of sticks covered with phrynium leaves, in the shape of a beehive.

Pygmies, known as the Bushmen, live in the Kalahari Desert in Botswana, Southern Africa. There are also pygmies called Negrito in some islands of the Malay archipelago. No records have been discovered of pygmies in prehistoric times.

"Pygmy" is the word used to describe *groups* or *races* of people who are less than 59 inches tall. They are found only among primitive peoples. The word is used to describe a racial type. Thus a man from New York, for instance, is not a pygmy if he is only 46 inches tall.

THE LEVANT

The Levant is the name given to the eastern Mediterranean and the adjoining lands of Turkey, Syria, Lebanon and Israel. Levant means "east". The levanter wind is a strong easterly wind in the Mediterranean.

In English history the Levant was indirectly the cause of the Crown using customs and excise to raise revenue. The Levant Company was in 1581 given the monopoly of trading with Constantinople (now called Istanbul), the meeting place of traders from east and west.

This company claimed that it protected routes and ensured the safe passage of merchant ships. It therefore charged merchants duty on goods arriving in England. The Levant Company continued in being until 1825, but its power to levy duty was taken back by the Crown in the reign of James I. Customs and excise have been an onerous and unpopular method of raising revenue ever since.

SOCCER

Soccer is a corruption of the word "association". Since the rules of Association Football were laid down by the Football Association, formed in England in 1863, it can be said that soccer began in England.

Where football began, on the other hand, is a question impossible to answer. Various forms of a game involving the kicking about of a ball were played by the ancient Chinese, and by the Greeks and Romans. By the early Middle Ages several types of mass football, often with hundreds of people taking part, were very popular. Indeed, football's popularity led to its being banned for a long time in England as it interfered with the practice of archery which was considered necessary for the defence of the country.

The team game, which led to the formation of the Football Association, was born on the playing fields of English public schools.

Soccer is now one of the world's most popular and widely followed sports. It is particularly popular throughout Europe and Central and South America.

THE HERMITAGE

The Hermitage Museum, one of the great art museums of the world, was founded in 1764 by Catherine the Great of Russia in Leningrad, then St Petersburg. Leningrad is second only to Moscow in the Soviet Union as a cultural and educational centre. It is the traditional home of Russian ballet, has 13 theatres, one of the largest libraries in the world, a university and many academies.

The city has 48 museums. Of these by far the most famous is the Hermitage, where the collection of art of all countries and

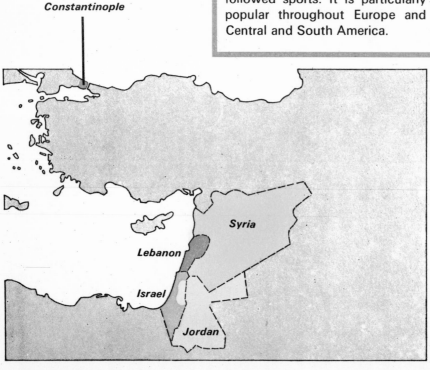

Constantinople

Syria

Lebanon

Israel

Jordan

is the Hermitage?

periods, especially that of the French Impressionists and Post-Impressionist painters, is considered one of the finest in the world.

Over the years, acquisitions by the Tsars and the addition of a considerable volume of works gathered over the past half century have contributed to the collection, which now includes more than 2,500,000 works.

The Hermitage was a private, or court, museum for many years until it was opened to the public by Tsar Nicholas I (1825–1855). It is part of the Winter Palace.

This splendid hall has a map of the Soviet Union in semi-precious stones. Above: a magnificent portico.

WHERE was Robinson Crusoe's Island? WHERE would you

CRUSOE'S ISLAND

Daniel Defoe's famous story of *Robinson Crusoe* (first published in 1719) is based on a real island— Juan Fernández. This island lies off the coast of Chile in South America and is now owned by that country. It was the scene of the true adventures of a Scottish sailor, Alexander Selkirk, who lived from 1676 to 1721.

Selkirk was born at Largs in Fife, became a sailor and, when he was young, took part in privateering expeditions to the South Seas, as the Pacific was then called. In 1704, he was the mate of the English vessel Cinque Ports. But he quarrelled with the captain and was left, at his own request, on the uninhabited island of Juan Fernández.

Before the ship departed, Selkirk begged to be taken on board again, but his request was refused and it was not until four years and four months had passed that he was rescued by the British ship Duke in January 1709. When abandoned Selkirk was left with clothes and bedding, firelock, gunpowder, bullets, tobacco, a hatchet, a Bible, mathematical instruments and books.

His powder soon gave out, but he learned to capture the goats on the island by running them down. He built himself a shelter and made clothes from the goats' skins. Fortunately, Juan Fernández never has very severe weather—only a little frost and hail in June and July (winter in the Southern Hemisphere). It is hot in the summer, but never unbearably so.

Selkirk found his island infested with rats, but kept down their numbers round his shelter by taming the stray cats whose ancestors had been left on the island by visiting ships.

He kept healthy and sane by working hard and by making companions of animals. But when he was rescued, he could scarcely make himself understood by the crew of the Duke, and he had lost all taste for civilized food and drink. He returned to England in 1711 and followed the life of the sea until his death.

CATACOMBS

The most famous catacombs in the world are to be found in Rome. The word catacomb is of unknown origin, and describes subterranean cemeteries composed of galleries or passages with side recesses for tombs. It seems to have been applied first to the catacombs of St Sebastian, on the Appian Way near Rome, which became famous as the supposed temporary resting place of the bodies of Saints Peter and Paul in the last half of the 3rd Century.

Catacombs are by no means confined to Rome. The custom of burying the dead in underground rock chambers goes far back into antiquity, and catacombs are found all over the Mediterranean world.

Most of the Christian catacombs—about 40 of which are known—belong to the 3rd Century and the early part of the 4th. Ruined by the Goths in the 6th Century and later by the Lombards, they were abandoned and their very existence forgotten until they were rediscovered by chance in 1578.

All the catacombs follow roughly the same pattern. Beginning as small private burial areas they finally became vast labyrinths of narrow galleries, usually three to four feet wide, lighted and ventilated by shafts spaced at wide intervals. The galleries led to small rooms called "cubicula" and the bodies lay in grave niches, cut in the wall or floor and sealed by slabs of marble or huge tiles.

The catacombs were used in times of persecution as hiding places, but there seems to be no truth in the widespread belief that early Christians used the catacombs as secret meeting places for worship.

Catacomb paintings provide the chief knowledge about primitive Christian art. They are also rich in early Christian inscriptions.

NUMBERS

The earliest written numbers we know of were used in Egypt and Mesopotamia about 5,000 years ago. At first men reckoned by chipping notches on wood or stone to record the passing of the days. Later the Egyptians wrote on papyrus made from reeds, and the Mesopotamians wrote on soft clay. They used simple strokes for ones, but marks for tens and up.

Three thousand years later the Romans still made strokes for one to four, but they used new signs in the form of letters for tens, fifties and so on. About the same time, the Chinese used a different sign for every number up to ten, but still used strokes for the first three numbers.

The Mayas in Central America invented the most remarkable system. They used only three signs—a dot, a stroke and an oval. With these they could write down any number, however large.

WHERE would you hunt for the Abominable Snowman?

ABOMINABLE SNOWMAN

The Abominable Snowman or Yeti is a half-human, half-ape figure of legend among the Nepalese of the high Himalayas. Nepalese mothers use the tradition of the Yeti to scare their disobedient children. "The Yeti will get you if you don't watch out" is a popular warning.

No one can say whether the Yeti actually exists. The first apparent confirmation of its existence came with photographs of huge foot-prints in the snow taken by Eric Shipton, the mountaineer, in 1951. Few people claim to have seen the Yeti and some believe it to be invisible.

Skins which the Nepalese say have been taken from dead Yetis turn out to be those of the serow goat-antelope or of the rare Tibetan blue bear. Tracks in the snow said to be the Yeti's footprints have proved to be those of a snow leopard, a bear, a wolf or a fox, which have melted to form the larger, man-like tracks of the Yeti. Nevertheless, the legend lingers and it may yet be proved to have a basis in fact.

PLIMSOLL LINE

The Plimsoll Line is a mark on the side of a ship to denote its loading capacity. Until a century ago many ships were lost as a result of overloading. These accidents were not only due to greedy shipowners insisting on too quick a return on their investment. Often a ship would be heavily insured, then overloaded to make it lie danger-ously low in the water. When the boat sank these speculators col-lected the insurance money.

Dismayed at this total disregard for human lives, a British member of Parliament, Samuel Plimsoll (1824-1898), agitated for a law to control this abuse. As a result of Plimsoll's efforts, the British Merchant Shipping Act was passed in 1876.

This Act laid down that every ship must have a safety line painted on its side. As long as the line is visible above water, a ship is safely loaded.

The deadweight tonnage of a boat is related to its carrying capacity. This deadweight capacity is marked by the Plimsoll Line, so the weight of the cargo and everything a ship must carry for a voyage is taken into account.

Load line marks according to Lloyd's register. These show the depths to which a ship can be legally loaded in different zones and seasons.

LR *Lloyd's register* **T** *Tropical*
TF *Tropical fresh* **S** *Summer*
 F *Fresh* **W** *Winter*
  WNA *Weather in the North Atlantic*

The draught marks on the bow and stern show the distance in feet from the ship's keel to the water line. The ship's draught is read as the average between stern and bow draughts.

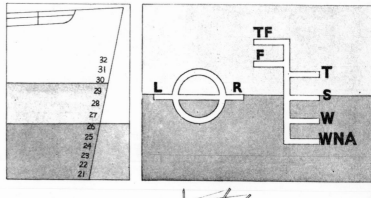

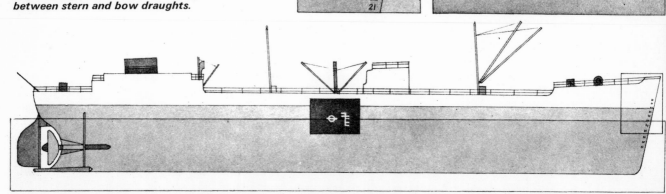

WHERE is the Plimsoll Line? WHERE do raisins come from?

RAISINS

Special varieties of grapes are dried, and are then called "raisins", the French word for grapes. Until the 20th Century they were produced mainly in the Mediterranean regions. Now huge quantities come from California and Australia.

Naturally produced raisins are spread out on trays and dried in the sun to a greyish brown colour. They have a tough skin and sometimes keep the bloom—the bluish powdery coating—found on grapes. But most of the raisins grown commercially are dried quickly in heated sheds and treated with sulphur to preseve them. These are usually small and dry and are used in cakes and puddings.

One type of raisin which is particularly good to eat is called Muscat. These raisins are grown near Malaga in Spain, and are dried in bunches, partly while still on the vine. These are called muscatels.

WHERE did baseball begin? WHERE is the Sistine Chapel?

BASEBALL

Abner Doubleday, later a general in the United States Army, was supposed to have laid out the first baseball field in Cooperstown, a village in Otsego County, New York State, in the summer of 1839 and there conducted the first game of baseball ever played. So strong was the belief in this story that in 1920 the playing field was established as a permanent memorial with the title Doubleday Field.

Doubts were later cast upon the story, and attempts made to prove that the game had evolved from the English children's game known as rounders. The name "baseball" to describe some popular English game was traced back to Jane Austen, who in *Northanger Abbey* (written about 1798) remarks of her heroine: "It was not very wonderful that Catherine, who had by nature nothing heroic about her, should prefer cricket, baseball, riding on horseback and running around the country at the age of 14, to books."

Then, in their attempt to tie up baseball with rounders, researchers came across *The Boy's Own Book*, published in London in 1828, and so popular that it ran into many editions. The book was about boys' sports and listed all the rules. The second edition includes a chapter entitled "Rounders" with a note that the game was called "feeder" in London and "baseball" in the southern counties.

As the game is described in *The Boy's Own Book* it bears a strong family likeness to modern American baseball. It was played on a diamond with a base at each corner, the goal or fourth base being the same as the plate beside which the batter stood. A batter might run whenever he hit the ball across or over the diamond. If he struck at it and missed it three times, he was out.

Many English immigrants to America in colonial times were from the southern counties, and it seems probable that they took both the name and game with them.

WHERE is the Cresta Run?

CRESTA RUN

The Cresta Run was built at St Moritz, Switzerland, in 1884 for the sport of toboganning—or sliding down snow-covered slopes and artificial ice-covered chutes on a sled with two runners. The sport dates from prehistoric times and was extremely popular in America and Europe from the late 1800s until the early 1930s, when widespread enthusiasm for skiing caused its decline.

The sport reaches its most advanced form on the 1,320-yard-long Cresta Run. Here the rider lies flat on the skeleton toboggan or "Cresta"—steel runners fastened to a light frame—and hurtles down the three-quarters of a mile of solid ice, full of steeply banked curves with expressive names such as "the horseshoe" and "the shuttlecock". The maximum speed is about 85 m.p.h. and it is a dangerous and difficult though exhilarating art to ride the magnificent Cresta Run.

Annual grand national championships have been contested on the Run since 1885. The sport, which is administered by the St Moritz Tobogganing Club, was included twice in the winter Olympic Games, in 1928 and 1948, each time at St Moritz.

SISTINE CHAPEL

The Sistine Chapel is in the Vatican, the centre of the Vatican City (*State della Citta del Vaticano*), which is the official residence of the Pope and the spiritual centre of the Roman Catholic Church. Situated in the heart of Rome, Vatican City covers 109 acres. It was granted absolute independence in 1929 by the Lateran Treaty signed by Pietro, Cardinal Gasparri and Benito Mussolini, then dictator of Italy.

The Sistine Chapel stands on the site of a chapel built by Pope Nicholas III. It was built by Giovanni dei Dolci, under commission from Pope Sixtus IV (1414–1484), who was a great patron of architects, painters, sculptors and scholars, and a great builder and restorer of churches. The frescoes in the Chapel were painted by Perugino, Pinturicchio, Ghirlandaio, Botticelli and Signorelli.

Under Pope Julius II, Michelangelo was commissioned to paint the ceiling of the Sistine Chapel. This magnificent work tells the story of Genesis from the Creation to the time of Noah, and took from May 1508 until August 1511 to complete. This ceiling is one of the world's masterpieces.

The Sistine Chapel is open to the public in the mornings, except on Sundays and Feast Days.

WHERE do these knives come from: kris, kukri, machete?

KRIS, KUKRI AND MACHETE

The two-edged Malay dagger or kris came from Java in the western Pacific. It was originally a one-piece weapon. By the end of the 13th Century it had become a dagger with a separate hilt of gold, ivory or wood. This hilt was carved to represent Vishnu's bird, the Garuda, the Hindu demon Raksasa, or Hanuman, the monkey-god. The blade became wavy to represent serpents or Nagas (dragons, spirits).

The kukri is used by the Gurkhas, who live in Nepal on the north-eastern frontier of India. Their soldiers are renowned for their bravery in battle, and there have been regiments of Gurkhas in both the British and Indian armies. The kukri is a sword with a doubly curved blade. It can be used to decapitate an ox with one blow, and was used with devastating effect by the Gurkhas on the battlefield, who were experts in hand-to-hand combat.

The machete is a common chopping tool used in tropical regions where the harvesting of such plants as sugar cane, maize stalks or hemp require tools which carry weight as well as sharpness. The blade comes in a variety of forms, but the basic machete is a plain and very workmanlike object.

FIRST OLYMPICS

The first Olympic Games were held in Greece, in a valley between the Rivers Cladeus and Alpheus. According to tradition they were founded in 776 B.C. After that date they were held every four years until they were abolished in A.D. 393 by the Emperor Theodosius I.

At first, the Games lasted for only one day and were for running and wrestling. Later they became a five-day event, and chariot and horse racing were introduced.

Well-trained young men came from all over the Greek world to compete for the prizes—crowns of olive leaves. Originally a religious festival held in honour of the Olympian Zeus, the competitors took an oath of honesty and fairness in front of the god's statue. The athletes took part in a programme of foot racing, boxing, *pancratium* (all-in-wrestling), chariot racing and *pantathlon* (five events of long jumping, running, javelin and discus throwing, and wrestling).

In the 19th Century, the idea of the Olympic Games was revived. After a break of 1,500 years, they were held again in Greece in 1896. Since then the Games have been celebrated every four years, except for 1916, 1940 and 1944 when the two World Wars were being fought. In 1924 the special sports of the Winter Olympics were introduced.

WHERE were the first Olympic Games held?
WHERE does all the garbage go?

GARBAGE DISPOSAL

Disposing of garbage is an ever-growing problem as populations increase. In country districts garbage is often taken outside a small town or village and dumped on a selected area of waste ground or in a disused quarry. What will burn is set alight.

A safer and much more efficient way of disposing of garbage is by incineration. It is put into huge furnaces, called incinerators, and burnt at a very high temper-ature. Everything is reduced to ashes, except metals which are collected and may be used again.

In low-lying areas garbage is sometimes used to build up the land to a higher level. It is spread out in even layers by heavy machinery, pressed down, and covered with a layer of soil. This process is repeated until a thick garbage and soil sandwich has been made. It is then covered with a final layer of soil and left to rot down. The land can later be used for farming.

In some cities newspapers and rags are collected separately from the rest of the rubbish. These can be pulped to make more paper. In other places, waste food is collected from hotels and restaurants, cooked and then fed to pigs. There is a growing tendency to find new ways of recycling raw materials such as plastics glass and metal, so that they may be used again.

ACKNOWLEDGEMENTS

The publishers would like to thank the following organizations and individuals for their kind permission to reproduce the pictures in this book:

Ardea 13 bottom, 24

BPC/Phoebus Picture Library Cover and 37 (Courtesy City Art Gallery, Bristol)

Barnaby's 56 bottom, 73 right, 78, 88, 95 (Courtesy Phillips Auctioneers), 96, 106, 124

Camera Press Cover and 65, 66, 67 top and bottom left, 76

Canada House 79 top

J. Allan Cash 60, 115

Bruce Coleman 12 (J. Bartlett), 13 (J. Brownlie), 14 (S. Trevor), 16 (J. Burton), 17 (J. Markham), 21 (C. Ott), 23 (S. Bisserot), 25 (J. Van Wormer)

Colorsport 3, 108

Colour Library International 41, 68, 69, 101

Cooper Bridgeman Ltd. Cover and 29, 109 left (Dedham Vale – Constable)

Mary Evans Picture Library 30, 31, 34, 42, 86 top, 91

Fox Photos 82, 119

Sonia Halliday 33

Michael Holford 45 (Courtesy Dickens House), 79 bottom, 121

Geological Museum, London 80

Iceland Information Bureau 67 bottom right

Keystone 38, 59, 94, 98, 120, 127

Frank Lane 15 top (R. L. Cassell), bottom (R. Thompson), 19 (T. Davidson), 22 bottom (Photo, Trinkhaus)

Mansell Collection 99, 126

NHPA 8 (A. Bannister), 11 (S. Dalton), 20 (A. Bannister), 22 top

Natural Science Photos 9, 112

Novosti 92, 118

Pictor Cover and 100 (Louvre, Paris)

Picturepoint 28, 36, 40, 53, 56 top, 57, 61, 72, 73 left, 80 right, 105, 113, 117 right, 125

Popperfoto 3, 51, 55, 62

Radio Times Hulton Picture Library 26, 27, 39, 43, 75, 102, 103, 110

Spectrum 2, 52 right, 54, 64, 77 left and right (also shown on cover), 81, 84, 85, 109 right, 111, 114, 116, 117 left, 123

Tate Gallery, London 89 (Experiment with an air pump: Joseph Wright)

James Webb 49 top

Illustrations by Ben and Stephanie Manchipp

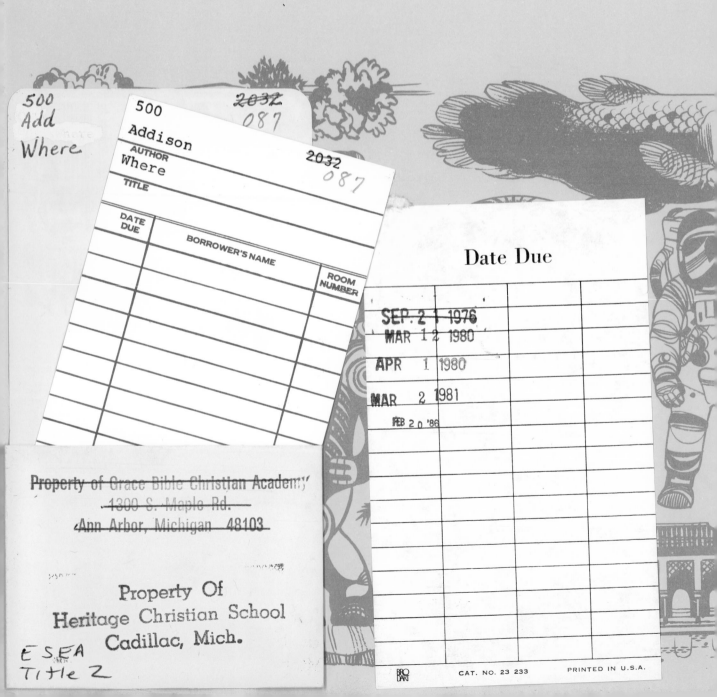

500
Add
Where

500
Addison

2032
087

AUTHOR
Where

2032
087

TITLE

DATE DUE	BORROWER'S NAME	ROOM NUMBER

ESEA
Title 2

Date Due

SEP. 2 1 1976			
MAR 1 2 1980			
APR 1 1980			
MAR 2 1981			
FEB 2 0 '86			

BRO DART   CAT. NO. 23 233   PRINTED IN U.S.A.